Big Bulletin Boards: A Cooperative Approach

Karen Robbins Bigler

Illustrated by
Laura Schmitt

Scott, Foresman and Company
Glenview, Illinois   London

Good Year Books

are available for preschool through grade 6 and for every basic curriculum subject plus many enrichment areas. For more Good Year Books, contact your local bookseller or educational dealer. For a complete catalog with information about other Good Year Books, please write:

Good Year Books
Scott, Foresman and Company
1900 East Lake Avenue
Glenview, Illinois 60025

Contents

Introduction

Teachers today have one of the most important jobs of all: educating our children. Along with teaching the many subjects in the curriculum, they must also teach values and morals, as well as attending to the child's physical, emotional, social, and intellectual needs. Because teachers have such an enormous job, they have very little time to brighten the classroom environment. The environment, however, is an important factor. Did you know that the atmosphere of the classroom may either inspire or stifle learning? It is possible to purchase commercial bulletin board materials, but I believe that it is much better to display the *children's* work in the classroom.

Content

In this book you will find directions for creating forty-two bulletin boards that can all be made by children! The boards, which are quick and easy to prepare, are very successful. Girls and boys in grades K–5 will all enjoy making these clever boards. Each student will be enriched by feelings of success and accomplishment.

Purpose

Making bulletin boards provides a fun, relaxed learning activity, while at the same time teaching many subjects in the curriculum. Of most importance, as the children work together to combine their artistic efforts, they will learn the value of cooperation, an important skill to have in this competitive world. In this way, the children will learn how much they can accomplish by sharing and working together.

Organization of the Bulletin Board Projects

The bulletin board projects are arranged from September through June, with four bulletin boards for each month except December and June, each of which has five. The teaching objectives are clearly defined, and the materials needed are listed separately from the text. The directions for making and for assembling the bulletin boards follow the list.

Art Media and Techniques

The art media and techniques list on pages 3–4 of the Introduction presents twenty-three different forms of art media and skills to which students will be introduced. At the same time, students will be provided with an opportunity to learn cooperation, develop creativity, and gain in academic areas. Each student will have an opportunity not only to enhance art skills but also to strengthen their ability in language, mathematics, physical coordination, science, and social studies.

Acknowledgments

I would like to thank the students, teachers, staff, and parents of Sunset Elementary School, in University Place School District, Tacoma, Washington, for their cooperation and support. Many of the enclosed bulletin boards were successfully created by students at Sunset School.

Objectives List, Helpful Suggestions, Art Media and Techniques, and Art Materials List

Objectives

Following is a list of teaching objectives that are accomplished in creating the bulletin boards:
- To develop creativity
- To develop small muscle coordination
- To teach cooperation
- To teach the holidays that occur throughout the year
- To provide a happy, pleasing environment for the stimulation of learning
- To create a feeling of success and satisfaction in art activity
- To provide a relaxed activity to teach many areas of the curriculum, such as mathematics, social studies, science, language, art, physical education

Helpful Suggestions

Here are some suggestions to help ensure success in making the bulletin boards:
- Plan early, collecting or making the artwork before the first day of each month. Then the bulletin boards should be displayed for the entire month.
- Always assemble the boards after school hours, not when the children are in the classroom. Children can never get enough of your attention.
- Invite students from the upper grades to help you assemble the bulletin boards after school. They love to help, usually acquiring rewarding feelings of self-worth. Teaching aides or volunteers can also be used.
- The appearance of many bulletin boards will be enhanced by first placing butcher paper on the board for a background. Choose the color carefully. Tan, white, or cork boards provide a natural background that do not usually need to be covered.
- Sometimes it is fun to surprise your students. Present the art activity without telling them what you plan to make from their artwork.
- Students can easily make borders to outline the edge of the bulletin board by using the borders on pages 91–92.
- Patterns are also provided for your convenience. Refer to pages 91–92 for quick and easy reproduction.

Art Media and Techniques

Following is a list of the various art media and techniques used in the creation of the bulletin boards:
  1. Trace and cut

2. Paper chains (different colors, different sizes, no-paste paper chain, and pasted chain)
3. Three-dimensional art form
4. Garlands (fold and cut)
5. Crayon resist
6. Tissue twist
7. Tie collection
8. Handprints (trace, trace and cut, painted hands, cut and curl)
9. Egg carton cutouts
10. Trace, cut, and yarn lace
11. Creative cutting
12. Glue and salt
13. Paper weaving
14. Cracked eggshell glue
15. Feet animals
16. Stuffed paper
17. Panty hose
18. Printing (fruit, vegetable, blot, sponge, cookie cutter)
19. Tissue-paper collage
20. Napkin folding
21. Puzzle pieces
22. Paper strips
23. Styrofoam art form

Art Materials List

Collect and save the following items for preparing the bulletin boards by boys and girls:

Adhesives and Tapes
Glue
Masking tape
Paste
Safety pins
Straight pins
Transparent tape
Wheat paste

Containers
Egg cartons
Grocery bags
Styrofoam meat trays

Fabric
Burlap
Cotton
Felt
Macrame
Material scraps
String
Thread
Yarn

Food
Apples
Eggshells
Food coloring
Potatoes
Salt

Markers
Crayons
Magic markers
Pencils
Poster paint

Miscellaneous
Aluminum foil
Knife
Lipstick
Magazines
Men's ties
Paint brushes
Panty hose
Paper plates
Pipe cleaners
Rouge

Wiggly eyes
Wire coat hangers

Paper
Butcher paper
Cellophane
Construction paper
Crepe paper
Napkins
Newspapers
Notebook paper
Poster paper
Tagboard

Tissue paper
Toilet tissue
Typing paper

School Supplies
Paper cutter
Paper punch
Ruler
Scissors
Stapler
Yardstick
Yarn needles

Back to School: Trace and Cut

Teaching Objectives

Emotional:
To welcome children to school; to build self-esteem

Knowledge:
To introduce subjects to students

Language:
To identify names

Materials Needed

Construction paper
  (red, yellow, blue, gray)
White crayon
Marking pen
Stapler
Scissors
Pencil

Directions to Make

This board may be made on the first day of school or by the teacher the day before. It's a wonderful way to welcome each student to your room and to discuss the subjects that are to be taught.

Using blue construction paper and the patterns in the border and pattern section on page 91 at the end of the book, trace around the boy and girl to make the correct number of students enrolled in your class. Cut out the traced forms and then draw on white lines for detail. Write a student's name on each figure. Cut out an old-fashioned schoolhouse from the red construction paper and cement steps from the gray paper. From the yellow construction paper, cut out a bell and attach it to the top of the school-house. Write subjects to study this year on each step leading to the little schoolhouse door.

Directions to Assemble

Your students will feel welcome immediately when they see their names on the children running to school. This bulletin board will also introduce students to the many subjects they'll cover this year. To assemble, staple the schoolhouse in the center of the board, leaving room below for the steps. Attach first the steps and then the children running to school from each side. Let's hope that everyone is as excited about school as these children are! Make this a really great year for learning!

September
Apple Basket: Apple Printing and Paper Weaving

Teaching Objectives

Art:
To teach paper weaving and apple printing

Language:
To teach vocabulary: *in, out, under, over, weave, basket, apple, red, white*

Physical:
To improve small motor skills

Materials Needed

Construction paper, 9″ × 12″ (red, brown, green, neutral or gold, and white)
White poster paint (thick)
Real apples for printing
Knife
Scissors
Paste
Paper cutter (teacher to use)
Stapler

Directions to Make

Using a 9 inch by 12 inch red sheet of construction paper, have children make several apple prints (with a knife, carefully cut the apples in half lengthwise), using thick white poster paint. Let the prints dry. Trace around the apple pattern in the border and pattern section on page 91 at the end of the book and cut. Then cut out the stem from the brown paper and two leaves from the green paper, pasting at the top.

Since children love to paper weave, they will be thrilled to see the finished, large wicker apple basket. Prepare 9 inch by 12 inch gold grids and about two hundred white 1 inch by 9 inch strips, using a paper cutter. Demonstrate paper weaving to the class, using a large sample at the chalkboard. Be sure to alternate over and under with each row.

Directions to Assemble

To make the giant wicker basket, first find the middle of the board, and then staple the woven paper mats straight across from left to right. Continue until all rows are formed. Curve the corners in at the bottom of the basket. Fold a few woven paper mats in half lengthwise to form handles on the sides. Staple the finished apples in rows, stacking them together. Oh, what a beautiful basket of apples. Give thanks for this year's crop!

Student Search: Game Chart

Teaching Objectives

Emotional:
To welcome each student to class; to build self-esteem

Language:
To help children identify their names

Social:
To provide a fun learning activity

Materials Needed

Bright butcher paper (color of your choice) large enough to cover entire bulletin board
Scissors
Ruler or yardstick
Marker pens
Masking tape
Stapler
Tape
Pencil

Directions to Make

Greet your new students this year with this fun learning game, **Student Search**! What a wonderful way to make each student feel like a special person and a part of the class as he or she enters the room.

Measure and cut butcher paper the size of your bulletin board. Choose a bright, cheerful color to coordinate with your classroom. You may need to tape two pieces of paper together. Using a ruler and pencil, mark off squares to make a grid to fill the entire piece. With a magic marker pen, carefully spell each student's name by placing a letter in a square (horizontally, vertically, or diagonally). Leave two rows of squares on the outside edge as a border, to add new students' names to the chart. After you have all the names on the grid, fill in the letters at random. Be certain to include the names of every student in the class!

Directions to Assemble

When you have completed the grid, staple it to the bulletin board closest to the doorway to welcome students as they enter. Provide a marker pen for classmates to find and circle their names. What a great way to take roll that very first day of school! When a new student arrives, add her or his name in the outside squares and welcome the student to the class. You're off to a great start in showing your students how much fun learning will be this year!

Students' Names Listed in "Student Search"

1. Dan	12. Les	22. David
2. Diana	13. Scott	23. Don
3. Laura	14. Heather	24. Andrew
4. Ann	15. Elizabeth	25. Drew
5. Eve	16. Beth	26. Tom
6. Earl	17. Liz	27. Brent
7. Dione	18. Lane	28. Dawn
8. Jay	19. Jeff	29. Dale
9. John	20. Darya	30. Violet
10. Owen	21. Josh	31. Noel
11. Ken		

From *Big Bulletin Boards: A Cooperative Approach*, published by Scott, Foresman and Company. Copyright © 1991 Karen Robbins Bigler.

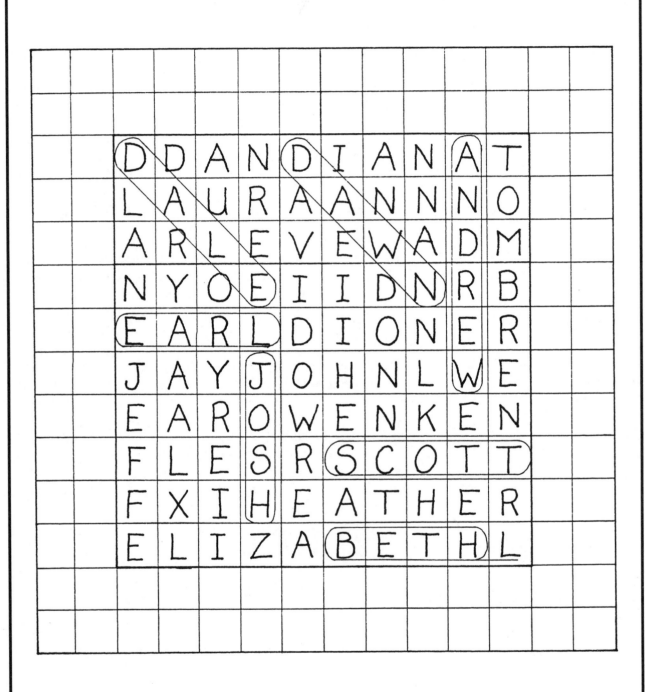

September
Football: Tissue Twist

Teaching Objectives

Art:
To teach pasting and tissue-twist collage

Physical:
To improve small muscle coordination

Language:
To teach vocabulary:
football, brown, team, sport

Materials Needed

Brown tissue-paper squares,
  2″ × 2″
Tagboard football shapes
Paste
Butcher paper (green,
  brown, and white)
Pencil
Scissors
Paper cutter (teacher to use)
Stapler

Directions to Make

Here's a great fall board that calls for teamwork. Cut individual football shapes from the tagboard, one for each student, using the pattern found in the border and pattern section on page 91 at the end of the book. Cut stacks of squares 2 inches by 2 inches from brown tissue paper, and place them one by one on the eraser end of the pencil. Pinch up sides, dab in paste, and place on the tagboard. Continue the process, placing each ruffled piece close to one another, until the entire football shape is filled.

Directions to Assemble

From brown butcher paper, cut out a football shape large enough to fill the bulletin board. Staple onto the board, and then starting at the left side, staple small footballs in rows. Place each football together end to end. You should have enough footballs to fill the giant ball. Cut and staple white butcher paper to form the bands on the ends and the stitching across the center of the ball. Add curled green paper grass for a touch of detail, if you like. You're ready to kick off football season and the start of a new school year!

From *Big Bulletin Boards: A Cooperative Approach*, published by Scott, Foresman and Company. Copyright © 1991 Karen Robbins Bigler.

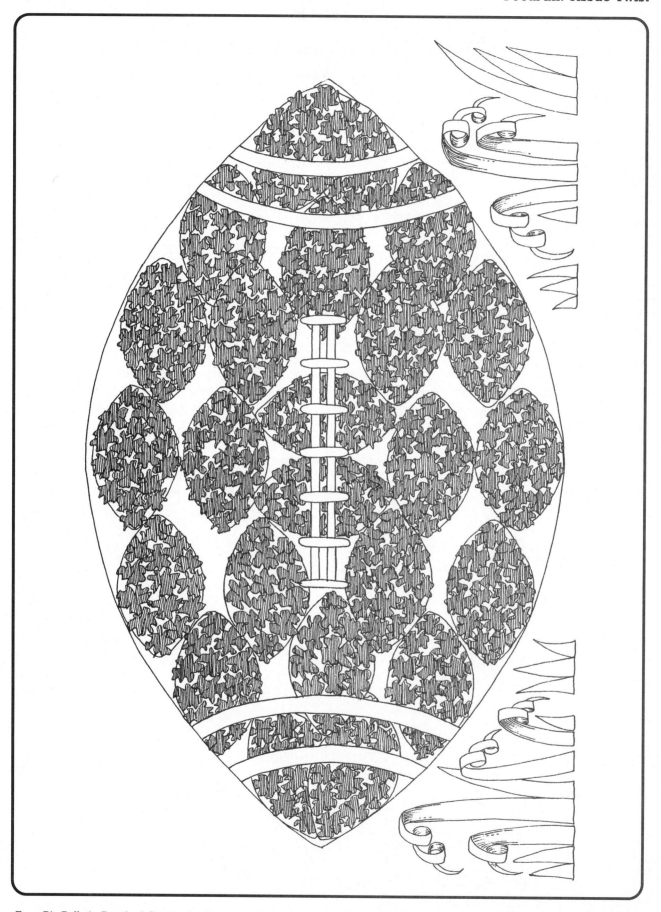

October
Halloween Pumpkin: Paper Chains (Medium)

Teaching Objectives

Mathematics:
To teach counting skills and the concepts smaller, less than, fewer, shortest, greater, more than, longest, bigger

Language:
To teach colors and color vocabulary: *black, orange, green*

Art:
To teach pasting and how to make linking paper chains

Physical:
To improve small muscle coordination

Materials Needed

Orange paper strips, 1″ × 8″
Construction paper (black)
Butcher paper (green, white, and black)
Scissors
Paste
Straight pins
Paper cutter (teacher to use)

Directions to Make

Maybe you can't grow the biggest pumpkin in the world, but together your class can make one. Here's how:

Using a paper cutter, cut orange strips 1 inch by 8 inches. You will need approximately 200 to 300 strips. If there are any leftover strips, they may be used for October bookmarks.

Teach your students to make a linking paper chain by smoothing paste on the end of the strip and pressing the ends together to form a circle. Have children "hide" the paste underneath. Now poke a second strip through the center of the loop and paste the ends to secure them. Hold the ends together with fingertips until they are dry. Have students continue to make their chains as long as they like. Then have each student measure his or her chain and then join the chain together with that of a friend. Making paper chains is easy and fun!

Directions to Assemble

To make the biggest pumpkin in the world, you will need a large bulletin board. Depending on the color of the board, you may want to cover it with black or white butcher paper. Covering it is not necessary, as the pumpkin is effective on plain white, tan, or cork-colored board.

Taking the longest chains in the class, form the outside edge of the pumpkin by pinning the chains in place. Try to make the left and right sides equal. Continue to pin the paper chains to form the veins of a pumpkin about 4 inches apart. Keep your chain links even and symmetrical. Cut and roll green butcher paper into a stem and form curling vines. Attach some leaves to the top to complete your perfect pumpkin.

You can assemble your pumpkin after school to surprise your class with the **Biggest Pumpkin** in the world. A week before Halloween, once again surprise your students by cutting from black construction paper two eyes, a nose, and mouth. Boo! Happy Halloween to each of you!

October
Sock Ghosts: Sock Cutouts

Teaching Objectives

Art:
To trace and cut

Physical:
To improve small motor skills

Language:
To teach vocabulary: *ghost, white, toes, heel, foot, feet*

Materials Needed

Butcher paper (white and black)
Scissors
Typing paper (white)
Black marker pen
Stapler or paste
Pencil

Directions to Make

OOOooo! Halloween is coming, and you had better watch out for this ghost, or he'll jump out and say "Boo"! Children love to make footprints. They will be surprised to see a ghost made so quickly. Have each child place his or her stocking foot on a piece of white typing paper. Carefully trace around the child's sock with a pencil, emphasizing each scalloped curve in the toes. Cut the tracing with scissors, and dot in two small eyes in the heel with a black marker pen.

Directions to Assemble

Back your bulletin board with white butcher paper, or if you prefer, leave it plain. Cut an extra-large ghost from black butcher paper to fill most of the board, and staple it in place. Staple or paste the children's small ghosts all over the paper, peeking in and out. These little ghosts are so cute, how could they possibly ever scare you? Boo!

From Big Bulletin Boards: A Cooperative Approach, published by Scott, Foresman and Company. Copyright © 1991 Karen Robbins Bigler.

Tilly, the Triangle Witch: Tissue Twist Triangles

Teaching Objectives

Language:
To teach vocabulary: *triangle, witch, black*

Mathematics:
To recognize and draw triangles

Art:
To paste

Physical:
To improve small motor skills

Materials Needed

Black construction paper triangles, approximately 7"
Black yarn
Black tissue paper, 2" × 2"
Scissors
Pencil
Paste
Construction paper (cream, black, orange, and green)
Stapler
Paper cutter (teacher to use)
Butcher paper (brown, yellow, white)

Directions to Make

Here's a great way to teach the shape of the triangle, and also to create a new classroom friend for the month of October. "Tilly, the Triangle Witch" can quickly be made by forming triangles together. First, cut from black construction paper triangles approximately 7 inches to a side. Use a paper cutter for fast preparation, as well as for cutting black tissue-paper squares 2 inches by 2 inches. Teach the children the tissue-twist method by demonstrating the following: (1) Place the pencil in the middle of the tissue square; (2) pinch the sides up around the pencil; (3) dab the base into the paste; and (4) place onto the black triangle paper. Place the twisted squares close together, leaving only a little space between each. Continue, until the entire triangle is filled and fluffy. Have a group of children do the following: (1) Braid two long legs from strands of black yarn; (2) cut out facial features for Tilly—eye, nose, mouth—and paste onto a large cream-colored, oval-shaped paper; (3) cut out two big black boots from the paper; and (4) make a broom by rolling brown butcher paper for the handle and by cutting yellow paper into strands of straw for a broom.

Directions to Assemble

First, decide whether you need to back your bulletin board with butcher paper. Then, find the center of your board and place Tilly's head in position, allowing enough space for her triangular hat. Begin placing the children's triangle tissue twists together as shown in the illustration. Be certain to place each one close together, so that there are no open spaces. Staple each one in straight rows, alternating top to bottom to form another perfect large triangle for Tilly's dress. To make the small triangle hat, simply staple the tissue-twist triangle at the top. Make two or three rows, depending on the size to be proportionate with head and dress. Attach the roll of black butcher paper, and staple on to make the brim. Staple strands of black yarn for hair, and then add braided yarn legs and paper boots. What an adorable Triangle Witch, and what a wonderful new classroom friend you created all together. Happy Halloween!

From *Big Bulletin Boards: A Cooperative Approach*, published by Scott, Foresman and Company. Copyright © 1991 Karen Robbins Bigler.

October
Spiders in a Web: Egg Carton Cutouts

Teaching Objectives

Language:
To teach vocabulary: *web, spider, black, legs*

Art:
To paint

Physical:
To improve small motor skills

Science:
To teach about spiders and spiderwebs

Materials Needed

Black cotton yarn
Black pipe cleaners
Egg-carton cups
Black paint
Small, wiggly eyes or paper cutouts
Straight pins
Glue
Paper cutter (teacher to use)

Directions to Make

Here's a simple spider made from an egg-carton cup. Using a paper cutter, cut egg-carton cups into individual sections. Have children paint both the inside and outside with black paint, and then let the paint dry. Cut out circle paper eyes or use wiggly eyes and paste in place. Poke eight tiny holes in the sides of an egg-carton cup, and push in black pipe cleaners. Bend each of the eight legs to make a creepy, crawly spider to attach to the giant spider web.

Directions to Assemble

Only a spider can create an intricate web, but here's a simplified version. First, using black cotton yarn and straight pins, carefully pull the yarn out and pin it to form this formation. Next, starting in the center, pin the yarn loosely (curving slightly), and then loop and pin it in place. Continue leaving equal distance between yarn strands until reaching outside edge. Attach spiders by pipe-cleaner legs to the web, as if the spiders were crawling about. Let's hope these scary spiders stay on the web and don't get **you**! Happy Halloween!

Suggestions

Sing "Eensy, Weensy, Spider"; spray-paint a real spiderweb; and make a print on paper. Teasels spray-painted black are even more effective, should they be available. However, they are prickly for little fingers.

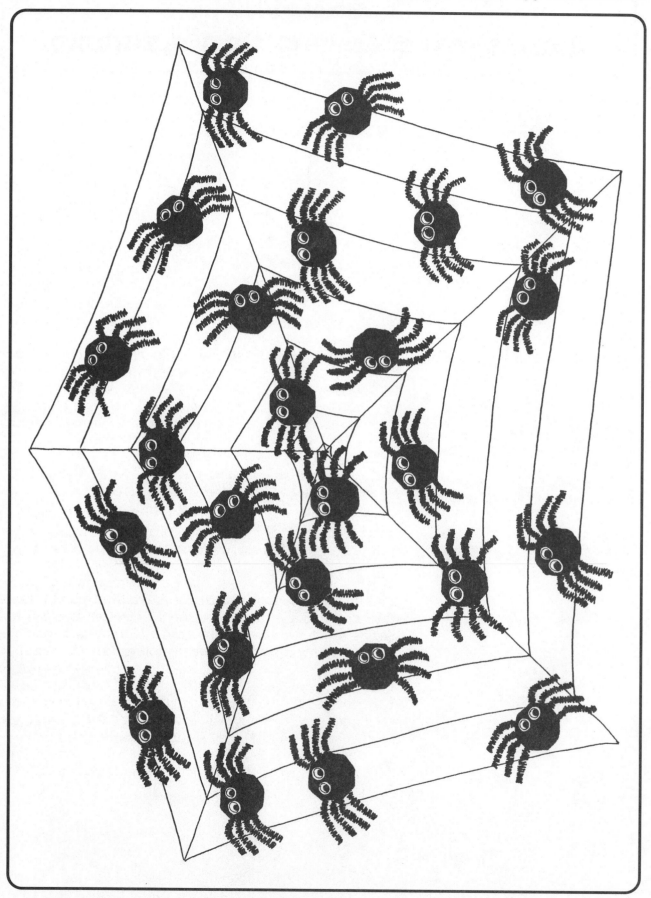

Thanksgiving Turkey (Mr. Tie Turkey): Tie Collection

Teaching Objectives

Social studies:
To teach the First Thanksgiving

Language:
To teach vocabulary: *turkey, ties, collect, Thanksgiving;* to practice writing names

Art:
To teach how to cut; to teach side view

Materials Needed

A collection of old, different-colored men's ties
Butcher paper (brown, tan, red, orange, yellow, black, and white)
Scissors
Straight pins
Stapler
Masking tape

Directions to Make

Who would ever think you could make the biggest turkey in the world from old ties? No, I'm not talking "turkey-talk." You'll be the talk of the school with this Thanksgiving board!

Simply ask your students to bring old ties from home. Be sure the students first ask for permission to use the ties. Show each child how to write her or his name on masking tape to label each of the ties the child brings. Alternatively, a piece of paper can be used to pin the label to the back side of the tie. At the end of the month, each tie can then be returned to its owner. Using the butcher paper, outline the following items: two long orange legs and feet, one large brown head and neck, one large red wattle, one orange beak, one white eye, and one black eye. Choose several children to help cut out the various pieces to form the turkey's head and legs.

Directions to Assemble

Start collecting ties toward the end of October, so that you will be able to assemble your Tie Turkey on November first. Depending on the color of your bulletin board, you may choose to cover it with butcher paper (white, tan, black, or yellow). Carefully place the head and neck off to the left side, and staple to secure them. Continue to staple on wattle, beak, and eyes. Arrange the ties to form the turkey's body, by pinning them in place. Start with the outside edge to make a plump, proud turkey. Continue to pin the ties close together, leaving no empty spaces in between. Arrange ties to blend together, forming a beautiful array of colors, patterns, stripes, and textures. From a distance, you'll think they are real feathers! Staple the long, orange legs in place. "Gobble, gobble, gobble! We're glad that it's Thanksgiving and that you're here to stay. This will be the best and happiest Thanksgiving Day!"

From *Big Bulletin Boards: A Cooperative Approach*, published by Scott, Foresman and Company. Copyright © 1991 Karen Robbins Bigler.

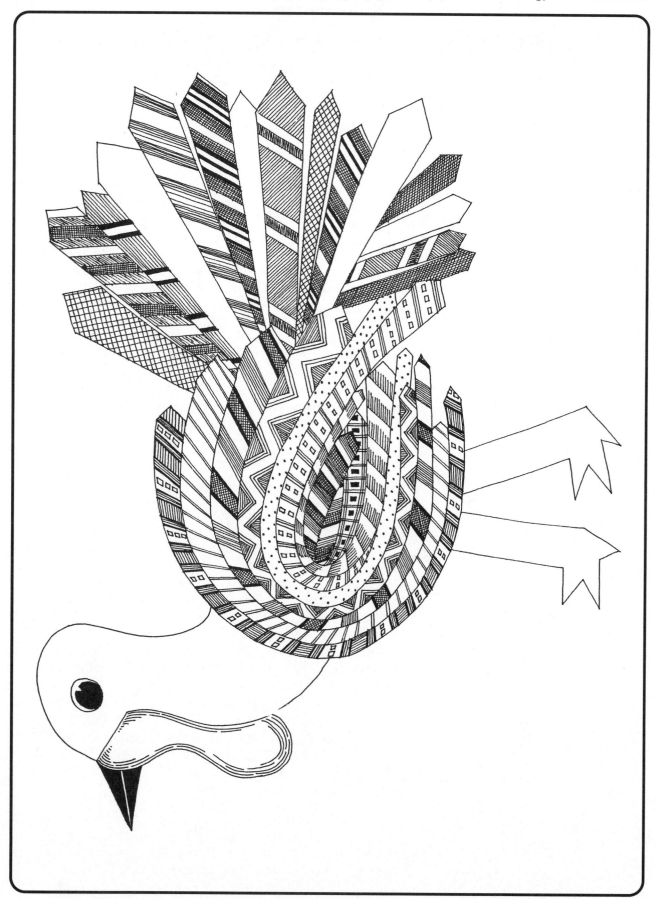

November
Indian Chief: Cut Handprints

Teaching Objectives

Language:
To teach American Indian symbols as written language; to learn coding and decoding

Social studies:
To teach about the First Thanksgiving

Art:
To teach how to trace and to cut

Materials Needed

Construction paper (red, orange, yellow, green, and purple)
Butcher paper (dark brown)
Black yarn
White tagboard
Black magic marker pen
Scissors
Pencil
Stapler

Directions to Make

Chief Tahoma will be a wonderful new friend in the classroom this month, while teaching your students about the First Thanksgiving in America. Have students make a particular color of handprints from red, orange, yellow, green, and purple construction paper. With a pencil, trace around hands onto the paper and carefully cut, following the lines. Choose a committee to help make these features: two eyes, nose, mouth, headband cut out and decorated by magic marker with imaginary Indian symbols, and two braids of yarn for the hair. Make a ditto copy of the imaginary Indian symbols which follow for students to decode the message (Happy Thanksgiving). Write other letters throughout the month, using the imaginary Indian symbols on white tagboard. This is an excellent lesson to use in teaching the history of written language to your class.

A =   H =   O =   V =
B =   I =   P =   W =
C =   J =   Q =   X =
D =   K =   R =   Y =
E =   L =   S =   Z =
F =   M =   T =
G =   N =   U =

Directions to Assemble

Cover your entire bulletin board with dark brown butcher paper, stapling to secure it in place. Slightly less than midpoint, staple the Indian symbols in white tagboard across the bulletin board to make the chief's headband. Staple colored handprints close together to form the various colored feathers for the Indian chief's headdress. Add eyes, nose, and mouth, securing them in place with staples. Attach braids at the sides for his hair. "How! Happy Thanksgiving!"

Suggestion

Write a letter, make a Thanksgiving card, or complete a writing lesson using the imaginary Indian symbols to experience one of the first forms of written language. Children will love coding all month long!

From *Big Bulletin Boards: A Cooperative Approach*, published by Scott, Foresman and Company. Copyright © 1991 Karen Robbins Bigler.

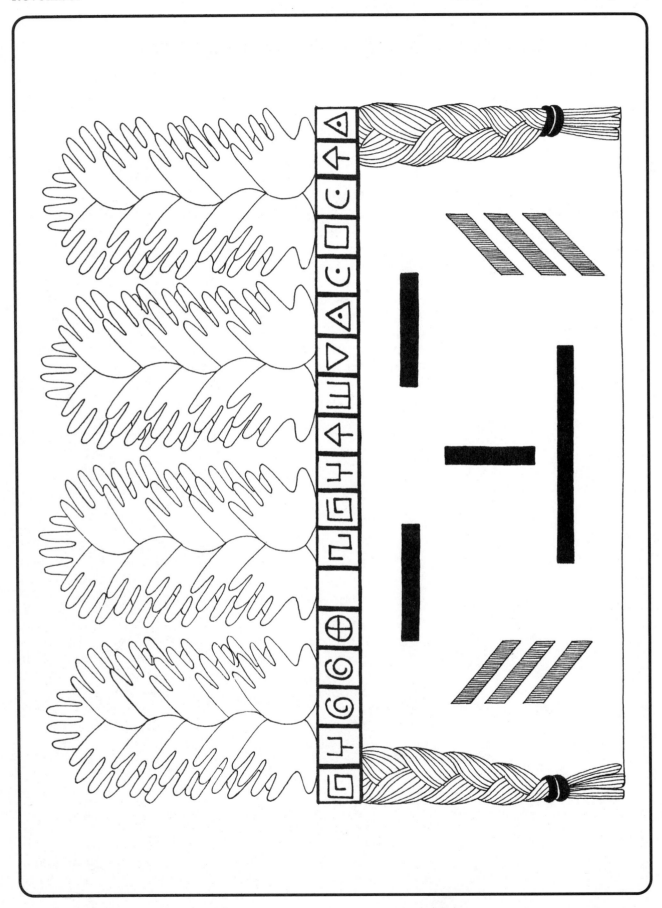

November
Pilgrims/Indians: Panty Hose People

Teaching Objectives

Social studies:
To teach about the First Thanksgiving

Art:
To cut and paste; to develop creativity and imagination

Language:
To teach vocabulary:
Pilgrim, Thanksgiving, feast, Indian

Materials Needed

Wire coat hanger
Old panty hose nylons (tan or brown)
Yarn (yellow, red, brown, tan, black)
Construction paper (variety of colors)
Butcher paper (white, black, and brown)
Glue
Scissors
Tape
Magic marker pens (various colors)
Rouge or lipstick
Magazines
String
Stapler

Directions to Make

Here's a wonderful art activity to introduce when teaching about the First Thanksgiving. Ask the children to bring clean, used panty hose from home, along with a wire coat hanger. Bend the coat hanger into an oval shape and carefully pull panty hose over it. Gather ends together and secure with string. Using the patterns in the pattern section at the end of the book, cut a hat and collar from construction paper, pasting to secure. Next, cut and paste facial features (eyes, nose, and mouth). Using rouge or lipstick, dab on two pink cheeks, and add strands of yarn for hair. Both boy and girl pilgrims can be made by simply changing their hats. Oh, what adorable pilgrim people! Indians can be made by following the above directions, only substituting yarn braids and an Indian headdress in place of pilgrim hats. Cut brown construction paper for an Indian top, dress, or collar, and with marker pens color bright Indian beads to hang around the neck. What perfect guests to invite to the Thanksgiving Feast! Have the children cut food from magazine pictures to place on the table.

Directions to Assemble

Let's set the table and then pretend that it is the First Thanksgiving feast. Invite the friendly pilgrims and Indians to sit around the table, which is overflowing with food from a wonderful harvest. First, cover the board with white butcher paper, stapling it in place. Cut a long piece of brown butcher paper, placing it in the center. Carefully staple pilgrims and Indians all around the table to eat together. Staple the collection of cut-out foods from magazines, or make your own to place all over the table. May this be your happiest Thanksgiving ever!

From *Big Bulletin Boards: A Cooperative Approach,* published by Scott, Foresman and Company. Copyright © 1991 Karen Robbins Bigler.

28

November
Autumn Tree: Painted Handprints

Teaching Objectives

Social studies:
To teach about autumn

Science:
To teach tree parts (trunk, branches, leaves); to teach why the leaves turn colors in the fall

Language:
To teach words: *tree, trunk, branches, leaves, brown, red, orange, yellow, green*

Art:
To teach rules of painting

Physical:
To teach the sense of touch

Materials Needed

Large piece of white
    butcher paper to cover
    entire board
Thick poster paint (red,
    orange, yellow, green, and
    brown)
Pencil
Paint brushes
Paint apron
Black marker pen
Tape
Stapler

Directions to Make

For those who experience the beautiful season of fall, it is fun to take your class on a nature walk. Observe and discuss trees (the trunk, branches, leaves, and the beautiful colors the trees have turned and why this happens). If you do not live in an area where fall is a definite season, you and your students can make your very own autumn tree. Here's how:

Measure and cut to size a large piece of white butcher paper (taping the back side together, if necessary). Place it on a large, low table. With a pencil, draw a large tree, outlining its trunk and branches. Have your students take turns painting inside the lines. Be sure to introduce the following painting techniques: (1) Always wear a paint apron or paint shirt; (2) dip the brush into the paint can carefully, wiping the brush on the side of the can; (3) use small, even strokes. When all the students have had a turn and your tree is completely painted, let it dry. Mix thick poster paint (red, orange, yellow, green, and brown). Have each child choose a color, and then paint his or her entire hand, covering the fingers, fingertips, palms, and cracks. Talk about the sense of touch and how the paint feels on the student's hand. Allow each child to choose where to place his or her "leaf-hand" on or off the tree. (You may want to write small children's names under each one, using a black marker pen.) Continue until every child in your class has painted a handprint leaf.

Additional Idea

Instead of painting the tree, you may cut the tree out of brown butcher paper, and then staple it onto the white paper.

Directions to Assemble

Using helpers, carefully move your large autumn tree to the bulletin board, and staple it in place. Most will say, "Painting is fun, even if my hand did get a little messy." All of the class members will be proud of their very own tree. The tree will be safe inside the room, where the wind won't blow these leaves AWAY!

From *Big Bulletin Boards: A Cooperative Approach*, published by Scott, Foresman and Company. Copyright © 1991 Karen Robbins Bigler.

Star of David — Hanukkah: Yarn/Foil Wrap

Teaching Objectives

Art:
To teach how to fold, glue, trace, and cut

Physical:
To improve small muscle coordination

Language:
To teach vocabulary: *star, Hanukkah, Jewish, holiday*

Materials Needed

White construction paper (for cut-out letters)
Butcher paper
Tagboard
Aluminum foil
String
Scissors/paper cutter (teacher to use)
Pencil
Gold felt marker pen (wide)
Glue
Ruler
Stapler

Directions to Make

This shimmering Star of David will be an eye catcher in your classroom, while the students are studying and celebrating Hanukkah. It is quick and easy—and so much fun—to make. Here's how:

First, measure and draw onto tagboard an equal triangle approximately 6 inches on each side, making two triangles per student. Cut the triangles out with scissors. Using craft glue, carefully outline a triangle approximately 1 inch from the outside edge of both triangles. Carefully place string into the glue, forming a smaller string triangle. Next, tear a piece of aluminum foil slightly larger than the triangle and then cover the triangle, folding the excess foil flat in back. Press the foil with your fingers, making an indentation next to the string. Use a wide gold felt marker to color the outside edge of the triangles. To complete the Star of David, glue one triangle on top of the other, making certain to center them evenly on each other. Let dry.

Directions to Assemble

To assemble this sparkling Star of David, locate the center top of a large bulletin board. Place the students' individual stars in rows as shown. Staple each in place to secure. Be certain to place all the stars close together, attaching each point precisely in place, keeping the stars in straight, even rows. Add cut-out letters or paint on butcher paper background the words "Happy Hanukkah." What a spectacular star you have made by cooperating together.

Suggestion

Other media which will be effective include yellow tissue twist, yarn stitchery on burlap, sponge printing, cellophane or tissue paper mosaic, plastic straw sculpture, and crayon foil melt.

Christmas Wreath Tree: 3D Wreaths (Small)

Teaching Objectives

Language:
To teach vocabulary:
wreath, candle, green, holly, bow, Christmas, berries

Art:
To teach how to cut; to develop creativity

Physical:
To improve small muscle coordination

Math:
To teach how to use a ruler

Materials Needed

Construction paper,
   12″ × 18″ (green)
Construction paper (variety
   of colors)
Butcher paper (brown, red,
   and white)
Scissors
Stapler
Pins
Paste
Ruler
Pencil

Directions to Make

Children will enjoy making their very own Christmas wreath tree this year. Here's how: First, have each student fold lengthwise a green sheet of 12-inch by 18-inch construction paper. With a pencil and ruler, measure 3 inches from the folded line in several places, and then draw a line that will connect all the dots. Next, mark points 2 inches apart along the fold. Carefully cut from the fold straight cuts into the 3-inch line. (The cut slits will be 2 inches apart across the paper.) Apply paste on the underneath side of the paper, and overlap to the edge of cuts. You may also staple to secure. Carefully bend the paper roll around and staple the ends together to form a wreath. Stimulate creativity by having each student decorate her or his own wreath with bells, candles, stockings, stars, gifts, etc. Each wreath should be unique to its very own Christmas wreath designer. Cut out trunk and bucket from colored butcher paper.

Directions to Assemble

Look what happens when all the Christmas wreaths are put together: You can have the biggest Christmas tree in the entire school! Take each student's wreath and carefully pin it to the board. First, find the center top and secure one wreath with pins. Attach the next two wreaths underneath. Always keep the top wreath as your guide for your center line. Place wreaths close together in rows, keeping lines straight and even. Continue to add rows of wreaths, leaving room for the trunk and the bucket. What a clever Christmas tree made by each of the students cooperating together! Happy Holidays!

Suggestion

You may also make a giant wreath by forming the individual wreaths into a large circular shape. Add a big, red crepe-paper bow to the top to say "Welcome, and Merry Christmas!"

From *Big Bulletin Boards: A Cooperative Approach*, published by Scott, Foresman and Company. Copyright © 1991 Karen Robbins Bigler.

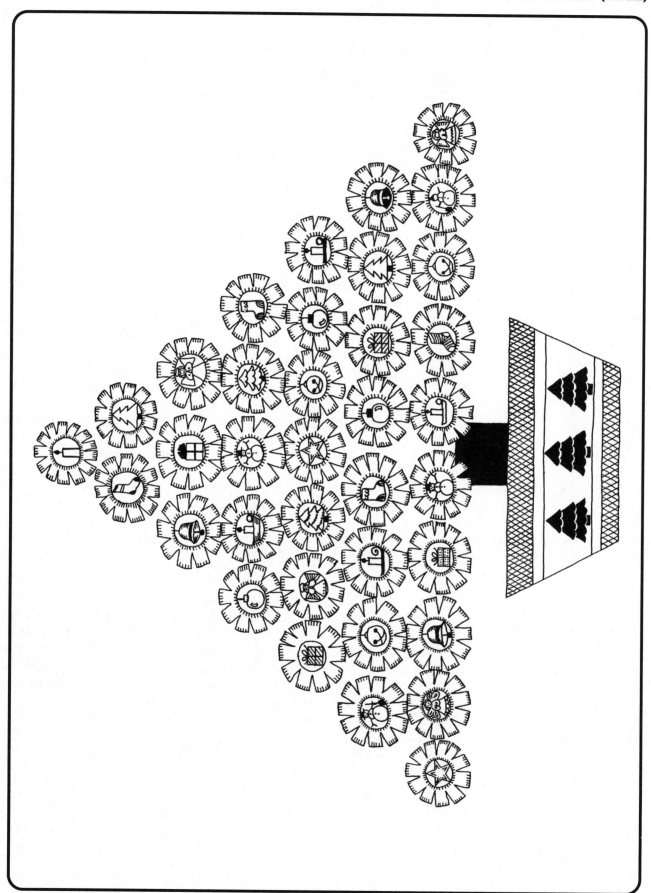

Christmas Stocking Fireplace: Trace, Cut, Yarn Lace

Teaching Objectives

Art:
To teach how to trace, cut, lace, punch, and paste

Language:
To teach vocabulary: *stocking, sock, Christmas, lacing, in, out, punch, red, white, fireplace*

Physical:
To improve small muscle coordination

Materials Needed

White yarn
Plastic yarn needle
   (optional)
Paper punch
Construction paper,
   9″ × 12″ (red)
White cotton
Butcher paper (brown and
   black)
Red/orange cellophane or
   crepe paper
Paste
Transparent tape
Tagboard
Pencil
Scissors
Stapler

Suggestion

Disassemble your board right before Christmas vacation, and tuck a surprise in each child's stocking to say "Happy Vacation!"

Directions to Make

It's time to hang your stocking "in the hope that St. Nicholas soon will be there." Children will enjoy making their very own laced paper stocking. How surprised they will be to see that you have formed a fireplace in the classroom!

The age of your children will determine the steps that need to be completed by the teacher (aid volunteer) or by the children. Begin by cutting red construction paper 9 inches by 12 inches. Using the pattern in the pattern section at the end of the book, make a stocking out of tagboard and trace it onto red paper. Hold two pieces of paper together and cut them at the same time. Tape the two pieces of paper together at the top and the bottom to hold them in position. Using a paper punch, punch holes approximately a half inch apart around the outside edge of the stocking. Wrap transparent tape around the end of strands of white yarn, or use plastic yarn needles, and lace the yarn in and out of the holes. Tape or tie off the ends, and trim the stocking by pasting cotton at the top. Be sure to write your name on the back of each sock. Surprise your class the next morning with this giant fireplace formed with their stockings.

Directions to Assemble

A fireplace formed with laced stockings perfectly gives the effect of bricks and mortar. Divide the stockings in half, because the left side of the fireplace must point to the right, and the right side must point to the left. The size of your class and board space will determine how many rows of "stocking bricks" you'll need. Leaving an opening for the logs and flame, staple the two inside rows of stockings on first. Slightly overlap the next rows of stockings, and continue to add rows until the outer edge of the board is reached. Starting at the right side of the board, staple stockings in place, slightly overlapping each one to form the mantel. Note that these stockings all face toward the right. Add andirons cut out from black butcher paper and logs cut out from brown butcher paper. Rolling the brown butcher paper into a log shape will provide a three-dimensional look. Flames cut and crinkled from cellophane or crepe paper will keep your classroom warm all month.

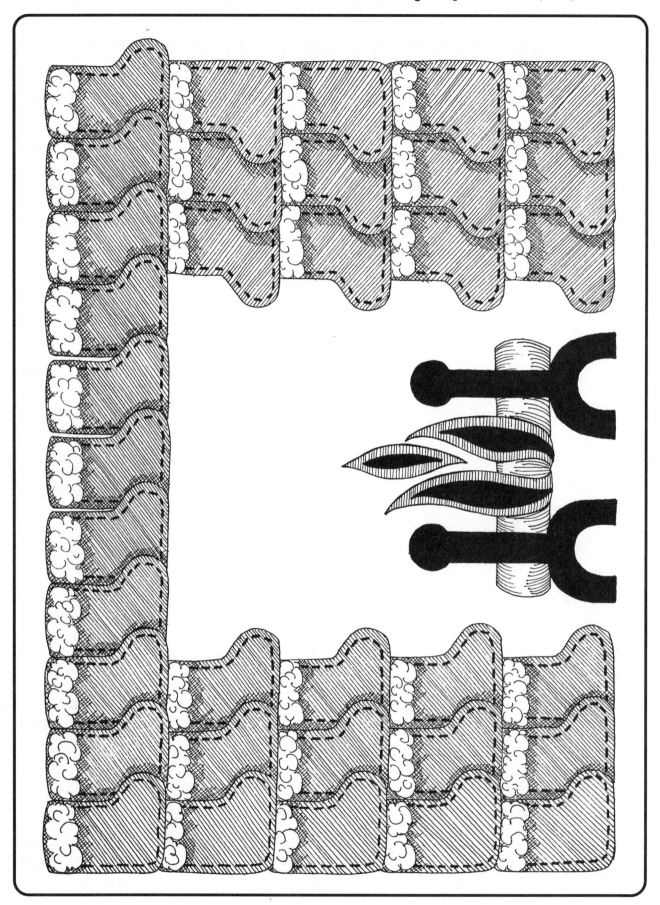

December
Christmas Stocking: Paper Chains
(No Paste)

Teaching Objectives

Mathematics:
To teach counting skills and the concepts: smaller, larger, less than, more than, fewer, greater, shortest, longest

Language:
To teach color vocabulary: *red, white*

Art:
To teach how to make no-paste paper-chain links; to teach how to cut and fold

Physical:
To improve small muscle coordination

Materials Needed

Construction paper strips, 3″ × 5″ (white and red)
Scissors
Pattern (optional)
Stapler
Paper cutter (teacher to use)
Butcher paper (green)

Directions to Make

Children of all ages will enjoy making this giant Christmas stocking and learning a new way to make a paper chain! The interlocking, no-paste paper chain, quick and easy to make, is less messy without the paste! Cut two to three hundred red paper strips 3 by 5 inches. Have children fold the strips in half and then cut from the fold, following around the outside three edges. It will look like a tiny fireplace. Continue cutting out a stack of squares, and fold them in half. Begin linking the chains together by keeping the first chain link folded closed. Open the second link and place it over the two open ends and press down at the fold line. Continue to place on another link by opening it up and poking one end through the open ends, pressing down at the fold line. Have children continue adding the links, counting, measuring, and comparing lengths with classmates. Have students add their chains with those of friends to make the chains longer. The size of your board and the number of students will determine the number of chains needed. Extra chains can be used to decorate the entire classroom.

Directions to Assemble

The stocking can be formed by stapling the students' chains to the bulletin board. The board can be covered with colored butcher paper. Begin stapling the white paper chains horizontally across the top of the bulletin board from left to right. Carefully secure the chain, spreading the chain links evenly apart. Place a second row of white chain links close to the top row, only reverse direction from right to left. Repeat process by adding three to five chains to form a rectangular shape to depict the cotton on top of the stocking. Next, add the red chain links forming the outside edge by stapling links at top left. Be very careful making this first outline edge accurately, because it will affect all others. Staple the links straight down and then curving to the left to form the toe. Continue curving in a downward direction, following straight along the bottom of the board. Curve upward slightly at the heel and then straight up the right side until you've reached the white chain. Carefully position the next chain links in line with the outside edge, slightly touching each one. Follow the lines, stapling to secure in place. Continue stapling the chains until the stocking is filled. What a fun way to make a chain, and what a cute stocking everyone made by working together in a cooperative way!

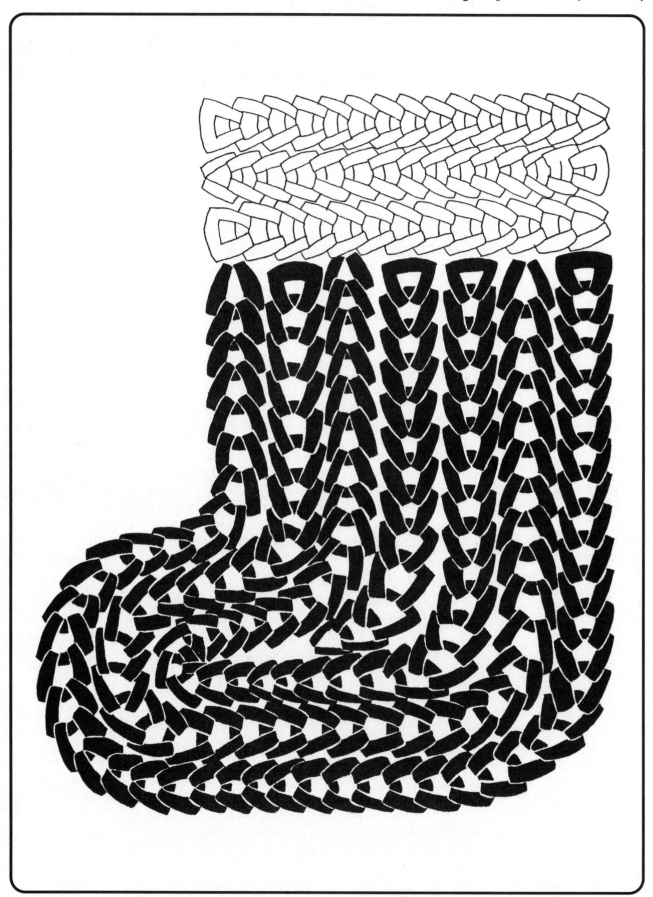

Christmas Tree: Curled Paper Handprints

Teaching Objectives

Art:
To teach how to trace, cut, and curl paper

Physical:
To improve small muscle coordination

Language:
To teach color vocabulary: *green, red, brown*

Language:
To teach vocabulary: *fingers, thumb, hand, tree, branches*

Materials Needed

Construction paper,
　9″ × 12″ (green)
Butcher paper (brown and
　red)
Scissors
Pencil
Stapler

Directions to Make

Hands are special and can do so many wonderful things! Did you know that green handprints can form a beautiful Christmas tree in your own classroom? Here's how:

Have children open their fingers and place their hands onto the green construction paper. With a pencil, trace around the hand and carefully cut on the line. Roll paper fingertip ends over a pencil to curl upward. Have each child make at least two cut-out handprints for the classroom Christmas tree. From the butcher paper, cut out a trunk and bucket for a tree.

Directions to Assemble

Your students will be so surprised to see this fluffy handprint Christmas tree! Simply staple onto the bulletin board the curled, cut-out handprints, starting at the top center of the board. Continue to staple on rows of handprints to form a triangular-shaped tree. Using first the brown and then the red butcher paper, cut and roll the trunk and secure the bucket at the base. What a delightful children's Christmas tree made by happy hands to wish everyone the merriest Christmas ever!

Suggestion

Children may enjoy trimming the tree by stringing white styrofoam "popcorn" (packaging material), adding a star for the top, and cutting presents from wrapping paper to place under the tree.

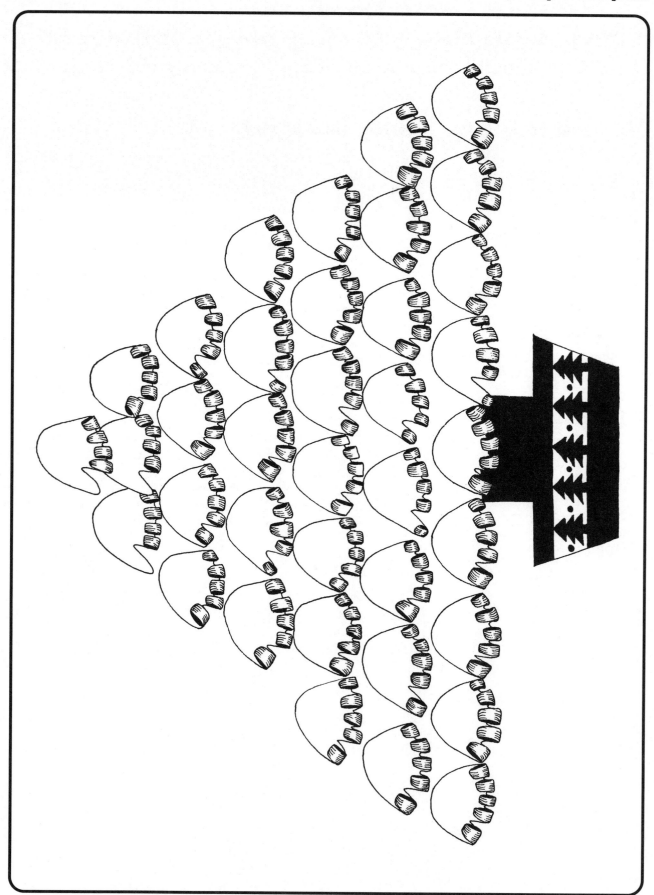

Teaching Objectives

Social studies:
To teach about the new year/old year

Language:
To discuss resolutions and provide group discussion

Language:
To teach vocabulary: *happy, new, year, resolutions, January, stork, diapers*

Art:
To teach how to fold

Language:
To provide writing and spelling lesson

Materials Needed

White paper napkins
Safety pins
Butcher paper (white)
Marker pens
Notebook paper
Pencils
Stapler

Directions to Make

Have this adorable stork fly into your classroom to wish your students a Happy New Year! The stork is quick and easy to make. It is best of all if the stork is made by the children!

Have each child fold a white paper napkin in half diagonally. Next, fold the left side into the center, then the right side, and then lift the lower point to the center. If the directions have been followed correctly, each student has just made a diaper! Attach a safety pin to hold all three pieces together. On a piece of notebook paper, have each student write her or his New Year's resolutions for the year and tuck them inside the diaper pouch. Either the teacher or a group of students may cut the stork's head, feet, and ribbon bow from the white butcher paper. Add details with marker pens.

Directions to Assemble

If you look closely, you'll see that the stork's feathers are actually paper-napkin diapers! Here is the easy way to assemble the stork: Staple the stork's head onto the upper left-hand side of the bulletin board, with his long legs off to the right-hand side. The stork should appear as though it is flying in the air. Take the individual diapers, stapling each close together to form the outer edge of the body. Be certain to keep upright so that the resolutions will remain within. Continue to place the diapers close together inside, until completely filled.

What a great Happy New Year stork made by your students. May this be the best **New Year** yet!

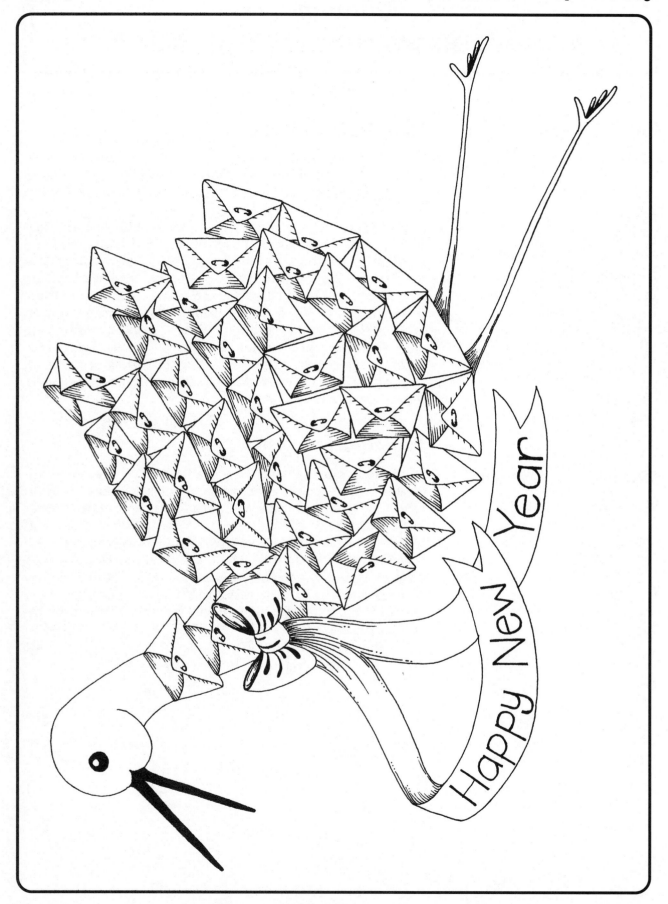

January
Snowball Snowman: Salt Glue

Teaching Objectives

Art:
To teach how to cut, glue, and sprinkle

Physical:
To improve small motor skills

Language:
To teach vocabulary: *snow, snowball, snowman, cold, white, shiver*

Materials Needed

White paper plates
Salt
Glue
Butcher paper (red, yellow, black, and brown)
Scissors
Paintbrush
Box
Stapler

Directions to Make

Whether it snows where you live or not, children will love making this cute, snowman friend. This is an easy lesson, especially for young children. First, take white paper plates, or white construction paper circles, if you prefer, spreading glue over the entire circle with a paintbrush. Next, with a saltshaker, generously sprinkle salt over the circle. (You may want to purchase the type of salt package that has a saltshaker included on the top.) When sprinkling the salt, place each paper plate in a small box so that the excess salt can be saved and used for other plates. Shake off the excess salt into the box and then let the paper plate dry. Have a group of children or teacher's aide cut out from the butcher paper two stick-shaped arms, a large hat, two big boots, and black circles for coal-black eyes and mouth; from the yellow butcher paper, the bristles of a broom; and from the brown butcher paper, a broom handle.

Directions to Assemble

Forming this frosty friend is just like building a real snowman! Staple each sparkly snowball close together to form a small head at the top and then a large round circle at the bottom for the base. Be sure to leave space at the top and bottom for the hat and boots. Staple on the facial features, stick arms, broom, scarf, hat, earmuffs, and boots. What a wonderful winter classroom friend for all to enjoy. What fun to build a snowman together—and one that won't melt away!

From *Big Bulletin Boards: A Cooperative Approach*, published by Scott, Foresman and Company. Copyright © 1991 Karen Robbins Bigler.

Igloo: Styrofoam/Salt Glue

Teaching Objectives

Art:
To teach how to glue

Language:
To teach vocabulary: *igloo, cold, snow, ice, winter, white, sprinkle, house, Eskimos*

Physical:
To improve small muscle coordination

Social studies:
To study different types of home structures

Science:
To teach about temperature differences, climate, and weather; to melt ice cubes

Materials Needed

Butcher paper (black)
Styrofoam meat trays
Salt
Glue
Pins
Paintbrush
Bowl

Directions to Make

Here's a great bulletin board to make this January while studying a unit on homes. Have the children collect and bring from home some clean styrofoam meat trays. With a paintbrush, have each child spread craft glue over the back sides of the trays. Immediately following, sprinkle salt from the shaker onto the glue and then let the glue dry. Shake excess salt into a bowl for others to reuse.

Directions to Assemble

To assemble your authentic ice house, pin the snow-covered meat trays onto the bulletin board. You may wish first to staple black butcher paper onto the bulletin board for background. Pin the trays close together, in straight vertical and horizontal rows. What a great igloo the children have made by working together just like **real** Eskimos!

Suggestion

When the month ends, disassemble the igloo. Have each student form the meat tray into a miniature igloo by cutting the tray into a semicircle and then cutting out a door on the flat side of the tray.

From *Big Bulletin Boards: A Cooperative Approach*, published by Scott, Foresman and Company. Copyright © 1991 Karen Robbins Bigler.

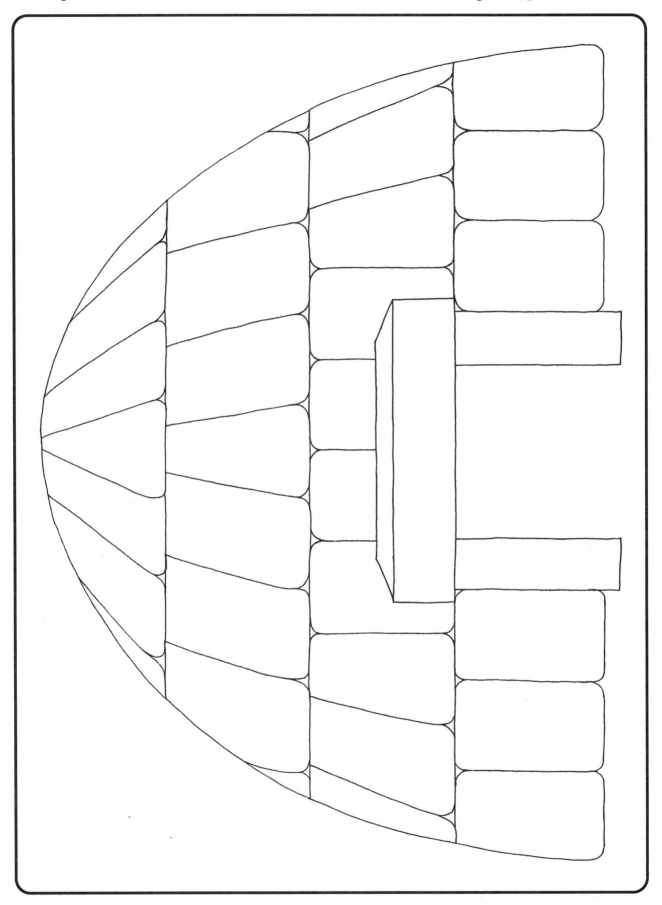

January
A Frosty Friend, Snowflake Snowman: Creative Cutting

Teaching Objectives

Art:
To teach how to cut and fold; to teach lines and patterns

Physical:
To improve small muscle coordination

Language:
To teach vocabulary: *snow, snowflake, winter, snowman, cold*

Social studies:
To teach the season of winter

Science:
To teach about snow

Materials Needed

White construction paper (typing paper or tissue paper is recommended for young children), 8″ × 8″ or the size of your choice
Construction paper (black and orange)
Cotton
Scissors
Stapler
Pins
Red crepe paper or red wool fabric for scarf
Brown butcher paper roll for arms
Tape
Glue

Directions to Make

Have an all-class project in paper-folding and paper-cutting to make this adorable snowman, which will be a welcomed new winter friend to the classroom. Children of all ages love to fold and cut paper snowflakes, but look what they can make when they cooperate and work together!

Children need lots of practice cutting paper and using scissors; this is a great activity to teach these skills. Have them fold each square of white paper into fourths and then cut out shapes, straight lines, and curved lines. The children should next open the squares and take a peek! Then have them refold the squares and cut some more, until they have made a delicate, unique snowflake! Each one will be different . . . just like each student!

Directions to Assemble

By taking the children's snowflakes and stapling them into three different size circles, you can easily make this lovable new friend. After the snowflakes are secured to the bulletin board, use the black construction paper to make a simple square hat, two big boots, two coal eyes, and button-like teeth, to be cut and then stapled or pinned in place. Cut a rectangular shape from orange construction paper and roll it diagonally into a cone shape for Frosty's nose. Pin it in place. Cotton can be used to make a trim for Frosty's hat by carefully placing a few cotton balls on the brim of the hat, adhering with glue if needed. Roll the brown butcher paper to make the stick arms, and pin on crepe paper or wool plaid material for the scarf. Use your own imagination in adding earmuffs, mittens, and so on. Since children can never make too many snowflakes, use any extras to decorate the rest of the bulletin board, windows, doors, or closets. Even if you don't have a real white winter this year, all children will love their new frosty friend!

From *Big Bulletin Boards: A Cooperative Approach*, published by Scott, Foresman and Company. Copyright © 1991 Karen Robbins Bigler.

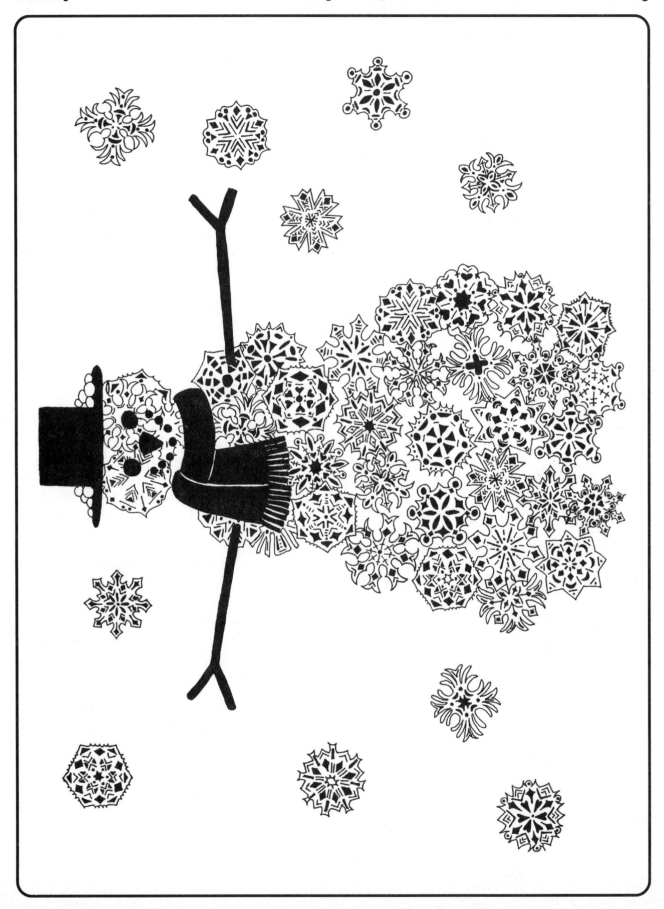

Fluffy Valentine (A Chain of Love Links): Medium Paper Chains

Teaching Objectives

Language:
To teach vocabulary: *valentine, February, mail carrier, post office, red, pink, white*

Mathematics:
To teach counting skills; to teach the concepts greater, more than, longest, bigger, smaller, less than, fewer, shortest

Social studies:
To teach about Valentine's Day, how it originated, and why we celebrate it

Social skills:
To teach the concepts of love, kindness, and friendship

Art:
To make linking chains; to teach how to cut and paste

Materials Needed

Paper strips, 2″ × 10″ (red or pink)
Butcher paper (white, tan, pink, or black)
Construction paper (white)
Scissors
Paper cutter (teacher to use)
Paste
Straight pins or stapler

Directions to Make

Together your students can make the biggest valentine in the world to wish all their friends the happiest Valentine's Day ever! They will have fun working together, making the "love links." Carefully cut red or pink paper strips 2 inches by 10 inches with a paper cutter. You will need over two hundred strips for a giant-size heart. To make a "love link," smooth a dot of paste on the end of a strip and press the ends together to form a loop. Hold the loop with fingertips until it is secure. Be careful not to apply too much paste (the paste should be hidden underneath). Thread another strip through the center, loop it around, paste, and hold it. Continue making your love links, and then join them together with those of a friend. See how long you can make them, being sure to count them as you go. "Who has the longest? Which is shorter, mine or yours?"

Cut-out snowflakes make a pretty white ruffle. If you prefer a lace ruffle around your valentine, simply trace your hand on white construction paper. Cut carefully on the lines.

Directions to Assemble

There are several ways to make this fluffy valentine. Decide whether you need to cover your bulletin board with butcher paper (white, tan, pink, or black) to provide a striking, finished appearance. Using straight pins or a stapler, begin attaching the "love links" in the shape of a giant heart. Place the links close together, keeping the left and right sides straight and symmetrical. To trim your valentine with fluffy lace, staple the cut-out snowflakes or the handprints close together to the outside edge. Oh, how pretty it looks! Happy Valentine's Day to each of you!

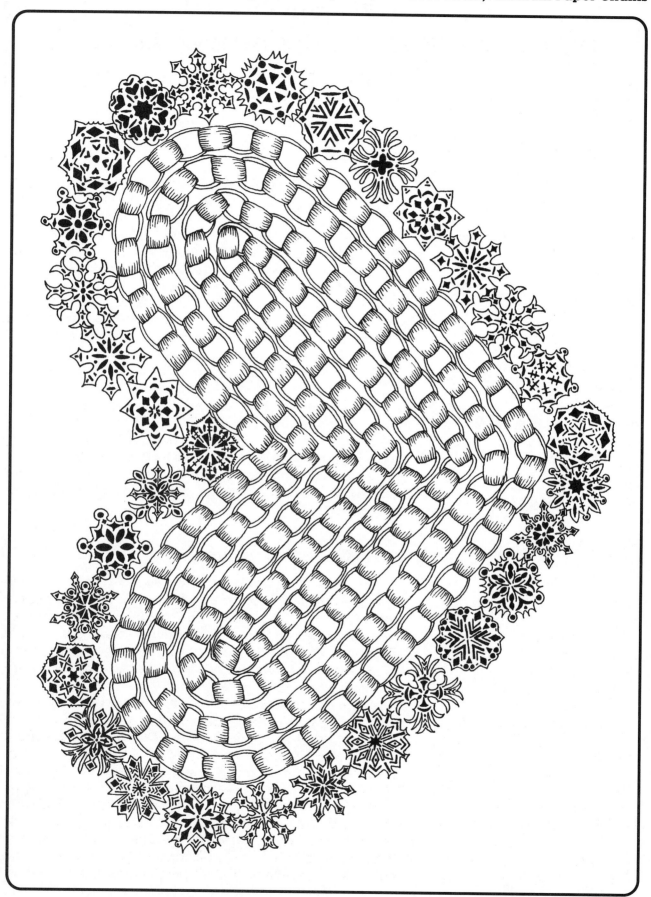

February
American Flag, Hands Across America: Cut-out Handprints

Teaching Objectives

Social studies:
To teach about the American flag, the symbol of our country (50 stars, 7 red stripes, 6 white stripes, and the meaning of the colors: red, *courage*; white, *purity*; and blue, *justice*)

Language:
To learn the abbreviation *U.S.A.*; to teach vocabulary: *America, flag, country, stars and stripes*

Physical:
To improve small muscle coordination

Art:
To teach how to paste; to make a tissue-twist collage

Mathematics:
To count

Materials Needed

Construction paper, approximately 9" × 12" (red and white)
Butcher paper (blue and white)
White tissue-paper squares, 2" × 2"
Pencil
Paper cutter (teacher to use)
Paste
50 white tagboard stars
Scissors
Stapler
Pins

Directions to Make

Children will love making this American flag, while learning about the symbol of their country. Be certain to teach the meanings of the colors of the stars and stripes as given in the teaching objectives, as well as what the numbers of stars and stripes represent. The hands joined together will symbolize the American people unified from one end of the country to the other, forming one great nation.

Have each child trace with a pencil around his or her hands on both a red and a white piece of construction paper. Instruct students to spread their fingers apart to make a wide, open handprint. With scissors, carefully cut out the handprints, following the lines.

To make the tissue-twist stars, you will first need to make a star sample and then to trace and cut fifty stars from the white tagboard. Next, cut 2-inch white tissue-paper squares, using a paper cutter. Place a pencil in the center and pinch together the outside edge. Dab the base into the paste and place onto a tagboard star. Continue until you have made enough tissue twists to completely fill in the star shape.

Directions to Assemble

To assemble, decide whether you need to cover your bulletin board with white butcher paper. (White, neutral, tan, and corkboards in good condition need not be covered.) From the blue butcher paper, cut a rectangular shape. Then staple the rectangle in the upper left-hand corner of the bulletin board. Be certain that it is the correct size and is in proper proportion to the handprint stripes.

Staple the handprints, slightly overlapping each other, with the fingers pointing from left to right, starting with the red stripe at the top. Continue to place handprints in straight rows, alternating the rows of colors, until all thirteen stripes are formed. Staple or pin the fifty tissue-twist stars in rows, alternating according to the correct position. Have the children join hands to form a giant circle and then sing "America the Beautiful" to the beautiful flag which they made by working together. May it remind us that in America it is recognized that all men and women are created equal and that all people are united together!

From *Big Bulletin Boards: A Cooperative Approach*, published by Scott, Foresman and Company. Copyright © 1991 Karen Robbins Bigler.

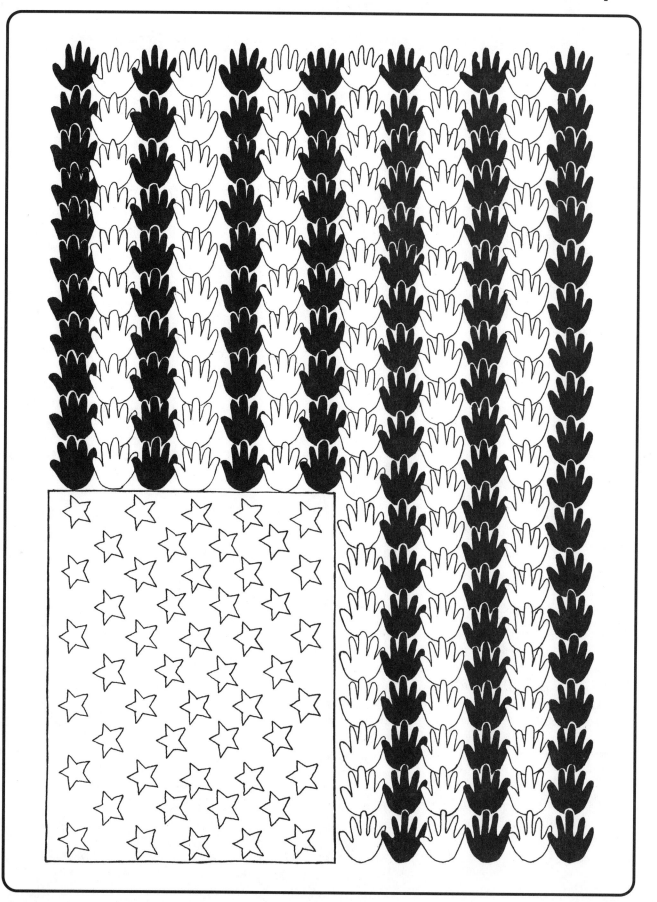

Heart Puzzle: Game Puzzle Pieces

Teaching Objectives

Emotional:
To build self-esteem

Language:
To provide a writing lesson; to improve spelling skills

Emotional:
To teach love, friendship, and kindness; and to provide a lesson of positive reinforcement

Speech:
To provide oral discussion of character traits and personality

Materials Needed

Large butcher paper (red or pink)
Scissors
Pen or pencil
Manila paper
Masking tape
Stapler

Directions to Make

Here's a valentine game to play while teaching love and friendship this month. Write the name of each student on the top of separate sheets of manila paper. On the back of each student, tape the paper with that student's name, and then have all the students write something "special" about each person on the paper on the student's back. This test of trust is a wonderful way to show each student's many positive traits, along with building self-esteem. After everyone has written on each student's paper, let the person read the many nice qualities others see in her or him.

Directions to Assemble

Take a large piece of red or pink butcher paper, and cut it into puzzle shapes, one shape for each student. Write a student's name on each puzzle shape and pass each piece to the named student. Have each student write on the puzzle piece, using his or her best penmanship, the list of "special" qualities. Have children help you assemble the giant heart puzzle and staple it on the bulletin board. Look at the beautiful heart that you made together, and enjoy the many *wonderful* qualities which make this class so special!

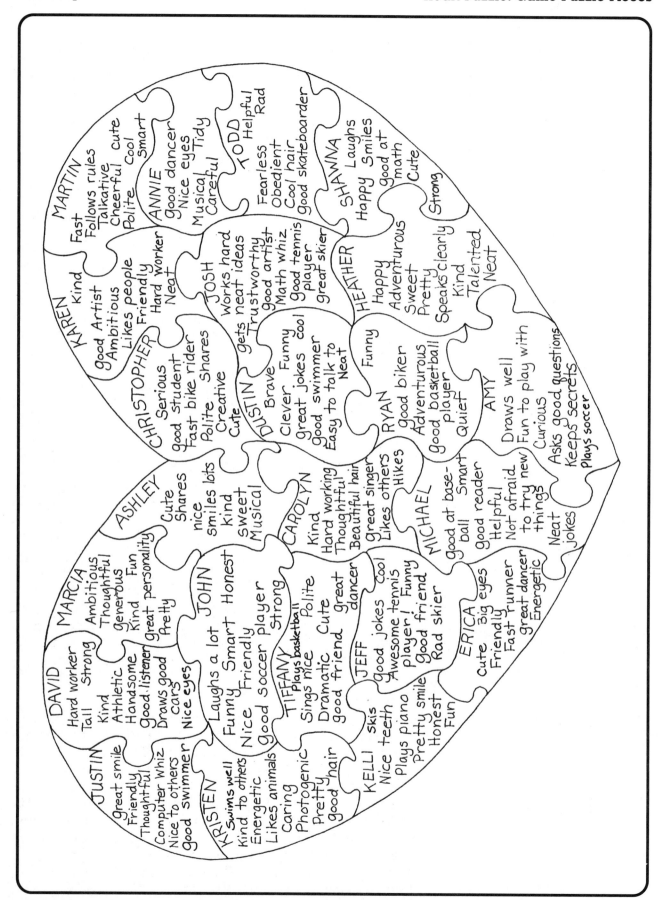

Teaching Objectives

Social studies:
To teach about America's symbol, the flag (the number and colors of the stars and stripes and the meaning of each); to celebrate the birthdays of two great presidents (George Washington and Abraham Lincoln)

Language:
To teach vocabulary: *flag, president, America, U.S.A., red, white, blue*

Art:
To make linking paper chains; to teach pasting and tissue-twist collage

Materials Needed

Construction paper (red and white)
Paste
Tagboard
White crepe paper for stars
Large butcher paper (blue)
Pencil
Yardstick
Stapler
Scissors
Paper cutter (teacher to use)

Directions to Make

Children of all ages love to make paper chains. Your students will feel proud to see what they can accomplish by putting all their chains together. By combining their efforts, they can make this spectacular American flag for their classroom and have the largest flag in the school! What a wonderful way to teach patriotism, particularly so in February when we celebrate the birthdays of two great presidents (George Washington and Abraham Lincoln). *Stars:* Determine the size of your bulletin board to estimate the size of the blue rectangle needed for the star background of the flag. Then estimate the size of the stars needed for fifty stars approximately 3 inches in diameter. Trace and cut out fifty tagboard stars. Cut white crepe paper into 1-inch square pieces. Pinch crepe paper over the eraser end of a pencil and then dab with paste and place on the tagboard star. Continue until the entire star is covered with the fluffy crepe paper. Let the paste dry before stapling onto the bulletin board. Continue with this process until all fifty stars are completed.

Stripes: Depending on the size of your board, cut red and white stripes of construction paper, about 4 inches by 11 inches. Have children work together to make seven large, long red stripes and six large, long white stripes. To make the chains, take a strip of paper and loop it around to form a circle, overlap the ends, and staple them together. Poke a second strip through the center of the circle, loop it around, overlap the ends, and staple. Continue to add more loops until you have the two lengths needed for the stripes in the flag. The size will vary, according to your bulletin board, so measure with a yardstick.

Directions to Assemble

This is a good lesson to teach children about the parts of our American flag—what the colors mean, how many stripes and stars there are, and why. Be sure to assemble your classroom flag accurately. To begin, staple the large blue rectangular butcher paper in the upper left-hand corner of the board. Be careful to make it proportionate to the size of the board. Then staple the three-dimensional stars onto the blue paper, alternating rows of six and five stars. Staple carefully the large paper chains, starting with the red stripe at the top. What a wonderful American flag you've made by working cooperatively. You can feel proud!

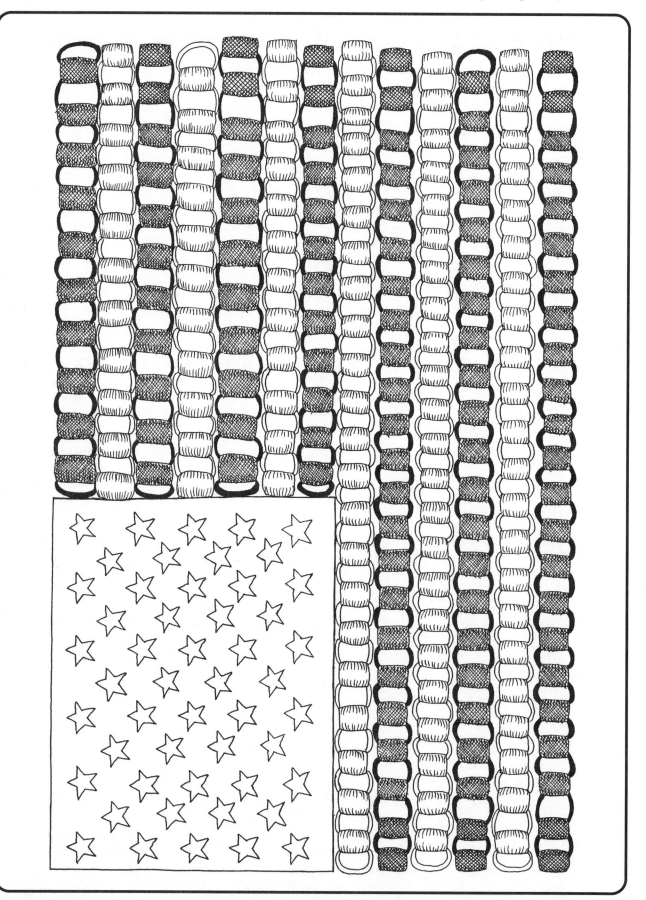

Teaching Objectives

Art:
To make linking paper chains

Language:
To teach vocabulary: *hat, shamrock, Irish, black*

Social studies:
To teach about St. Patrick's Day

Physical:
To improve small muscle coordination

Mathematics:
To teach counting skills; to teach the concepts of less than, more than, longer, shorter

Materials Needed

Construction paper strips, 2″ × 10″ (black)
Butcher paper (green)
Stapler
Paste
Paper cutter (teacher to use)
Pins

Directions to Make

To make this giant St. Patrick's hat, cut two hundred to three hundred strips of black construction paper 2 inches by 10 inches on a paper cutter. Next, take a strip of black construction paper and loop it around to form a circle, overlap the ends, and paste them together. Poke a second strip through the center of the circle, loop it around, overlap the ends, and paste them together. Should the loops not adhere easily with paste, a stapler is recommended. Have students continue to add more loops, and see how long they can make their chains. Then have each student add his or her chain with that of a friend, and then add that with the chain of another friend, until the whole class has joined all the chains together! Have students count to see how many loops there are in the entire chain.

Directions to Assemble

To assemble this giant St. Patrick's hat, start at the lower left side of your bulletin board. Carefully place the paper chains along the lower edge of the bulletin board, pinning in place as you go, to form the brim of the hat. Bring the chain upward on the right side and circle back to the left. Continue to pin chains in straight rows, until the brim is completely filled in. Begin to form the crown of the hat by pinning chains about one foot from the sides of the board. Circle the chain upward, curving it gradually, and then circle downward to the lower right side of the board, pinning it as you go. Continue to secure the chains in place following the lined pattern formed by the outer row of chains. When the hat is completed, cut from the green butcher paper a long green band and secure it to the hat. If you wish, add a shamrock off to one side. Here's wishing you the "luck of the Irish"!

From *Big Bulletin Boards: A Cooperative Approach*, published by Scott, Foresman and Company. Copyright © 1991 Karen Robbins Bigler.

March
Kids' Kite: Cut and Color

Teaching Objectives

Art:
To teach how to trace and cut; to develop creativity and imagination

Physical:
To improve small muscle coordination

Materials Needed

Butcher paper for sky
   background (blue)
Butcher paper for clouds
   (white)
Construction paper,
   12″ × 18″ (manila)
Tagboard kite pattern
Crayons or felt marker pens
Yarn
Paper cutter (teacher to
   use)
Stapler

Directions to Make

Using the kite pattern in the border and pattern section at the end of the book, cut with the paper cutter a kite shape from construction paper 12 inches by 18 inches. Have students design their own pattern, using crayons or felt markers. This lesson will challenge children to use their imaginations and work with a repetitive design.

Directions to Assemble

You may prefer first to back your bulletin board with bright-blue butcher paper. To form one large kite, carefully staple each kite in place, with each kite slightly overlapping the next, forming rows. When arranged together, the smaller kites will form a colorful pattern, making one large kite. Add yarn for the tail, and then add some puffy white clouds for your kite to soar through the sky.

Note: When you disassemble board, staple some yarn on each smaller kite for a tail so it can fly home.

March
Shamrock Plant: Printing

Teaching Objectives

Art:
To teach how to print and cut

Physical:
To improve small muscle coordination

Language:
To teach vocabulary: *green, shamrock, Saint Patrick's Day, flowerpot*

Materials Needed

Construction paper,
  9″ × 12″ (light green)
Thick green paint
Potato (or plastic
  cookie-cutter clover)
Green yarn
Butcher paper (brown or
  rust)
Knife (teacher to use)
Shamrock plant
Tagboard
Stapler

Directions to Make

Students will enjoy celebrating Saint Patrick's Day by making their very own giant shamrock plant. It may be helpful first to buy a small shamrock plant from a local florist so that the children can observe the delicate, green leafy plant. Using the pattern found in the border and pattern section at the end of the book, make a shamrock from tagboard, 9 inches by 12 inches. Have students trace around the pattern on light green construction paper and then cut out the shape. Using a clover-shaped plastic cookie cutter or cutting a shamrock from half a potato, dip the pattern into thick green poster paint, and print onto the light green shamrock. Continue printing until you're satisfied with your design. Let the shamrocks dry. Staple on strands of green yarn for stems. Next, cut a large clay pot from brown or rust butcher paper.

Directions to Assemble

To assemble the shamrock plant, first place the cut-out clay pot in the center of the bulletin board, filling the lower half. Position each shamrock to form a balanced arrangement, and staple each shamrock in place. Tuck the stems made from green yarn inside the pot, and staple down if necessary. The luck of the Irish to you on this Saint Patrick's Day!

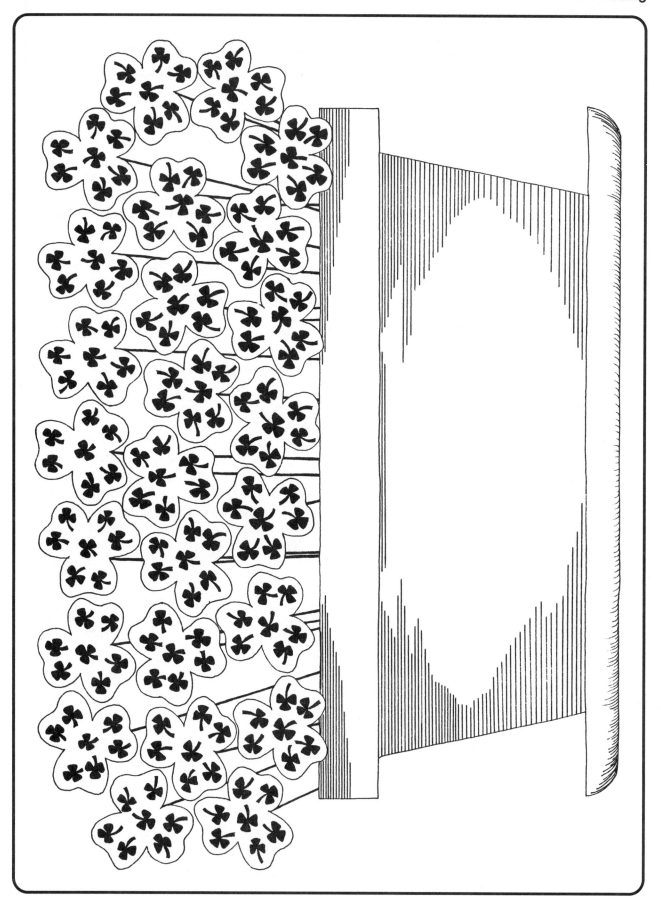

March
Paper Shamrock: Large Paper Chains

Teaching Objectives

Art:
To make linking paper chains

Language:
To teach vocabulary: *green, shamrock, Irish*

Mathematics:
To teach counting skills and the concepts less than, more than, longer, shorter

Physical:
To improve small muscle coordination

Materials Needed

Large strips of construction
    paper, 2″ × 10″ (green)
Butcher paper (green)
Pins
Stapler
Paper cutter (teacher to use)

Directions to Make

Children love to make paper chains. Look what can be made when paper chains are put together—a shamrock! Prepare two hundred to three hundred strips of paper 2 inches by 10 inches, using a paper cutter. Begin making giant paper chains by taking a large green strip of construction paper, loop it to make a circle with the ends overlapping, and staple the ends together. Now take another strip and poke it through the opening in the first, loop it around, overlap the ends, and staple the ends together. Continue this process, counting the chain links as you go. Have each student compare her or his chain with that of a friend.

Directions to Assemble

To make this giant shamrock, first join all the chains together, and then divide the long chain into equal thirds. Pin or staple the chains into three triangular shapes. Begin on the left side of the board, forming the outside line. Be extra careful with this first step, as it will determine all other rows. Continue to pin the chains close together on the inside triangle until you have reached the center, forming the first leaf. You will have made four triangular chains, decreasing in size until completely filled. Form the second and third leaves in the same manner. Using extra chains, form the stem in the center of the shamrock to complete. Happy St. Patrick's Day!

From *Big Bulletin Boards: A Cooperative Approach*, published by Scott, Foresman and Company. Copyright © 1991 Karen Robbins Bigler.

Feet Chicks/Bunnies: Footprint Cutouts

Teaching Objectives

Art:
To teach how to trace, cut, and paste; to develop creativity and imagination

Physical:
To improve small motor skills

Materials Needed

Construction paper, 9″ × 12″ (yellow, white, green, pink, and blue)
Crayons or felt pens
Scissors
Large butcher paper (pink, blue, and white)
Paste
Yellow yarn
Pencil
Stapler

Directions to Make

This giant Easter basket is packed full of Easter joy! Children will have fun making an adorable Easter chick or bunny by tracing their own feet. If time allows, have students make both the chick and the bunny. To make the chick, have the students first remove a shoe and place one stocking foot on the 9 inch by 12 inch yellow construction paper. With a pencil, lightly trace around the stocking foot. Cut out the foot image and draw facial features on it with crayons or felt pens. Glue yellow yarn strands on the head to create feathers. To make the bunny, have students place a stocking foot on white construction paper. Trace around the foot and cut out the foot image. From colored construction paper, cut out ears, bonnets, hats, and so on, and glue them in place. Add facial features with crayons or felt pens. Cut a cracked eggshell (see the illustration) from a large sheet of white butcher paper. To make the grass, cut and curl green construction paper.

Directions to Assemble

First cover the entire board with pink or blue butcher paper. Staple the large eggshell basket to fill the lower half of the board. Add the curled grass around the giant eggshell, stapling in place. Stuff the eggshell basket with the chicks and bunnies to bring a basketful of Easter joy! Hoppy Easter!

April
Paper Plate Bunny: Tissues

Teaching Objectives

Art:
To teach how to paste; to teach tissue-twist collage

Physical:
To feel texture; to improve small muscle coordination

Materials Needed

Construction paper (red, pink, green, and black; other colors for Easter eggs)
Toilet tissues (white and pink)
White paper plates
Glue or paste
Pink pipe cleaners
Stapler

Directions to Make

This giant Easter bunny will lead the Easter parade, bringing Easter cheer to all her friends. She's so soft and easy to make! Give each child a white paper plate and a stack of white toilet-tissue squares. Place a pencil in the center of a tissue square and pinch up the sides. Dab the tissue into the paste and place the tissue on the paper plate. Continue this process, placing each tissue twist close together, until the entire plate is covered. You may want to place pink toilet tissues in the center of the plates to be used for the ears and the feet.

Directions to Assemble

To make the giant Easter bunny, staple each fluffy white paper plate close together, forming two circles (a small one for the head and a large one for the body). Place several pink tissue plates together to make two hoppity feet and two floppy ears on top of the head. Add eyes, nose, and mouth cut out from colored construction paper, along with pink pipe cleaners for whiskers. Add a touch of curled grass made from the green construction paper and hide some Easter eggs made from colored construction paper to complete this adorable bunny to wish you the Hoppiest Easter ever!

From *Big Bulletin Boards: A Cooperative Approach*, published by Scott, Foresman and Company. Copyright © 1991 Karen Robbins Bigler.

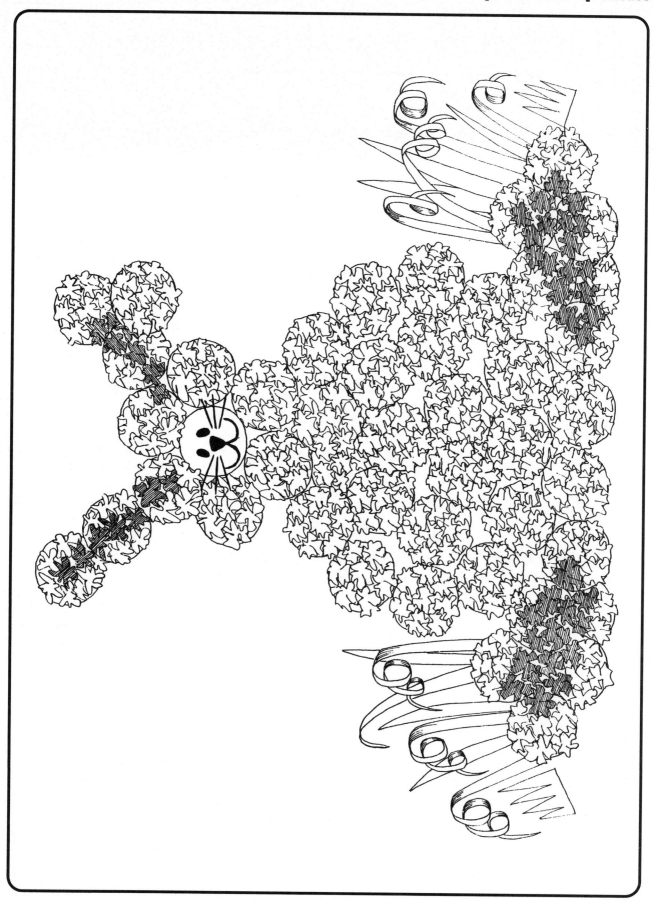

Giant Easter Egg: Cracked Eggshells

Teaching Objectives

Art:
To trace, cut, and glue

Physical:
To improve small muscle coordination

Language:
To teach vocabulary: *eggshell, cracked, glue, mosaic*

Materials Needed

Cracked eggshells (save and bring from home)
Food coloring (three different colors)
Tagboard egg pattern
Large butcher paper pastel color and white
Construction paper (green, and three different pastel colors the same as those for food dye)
Pencil
Scissors
Glue/paste
Grocery bag
Paintbrush
Stapler

Directions to Make

Here's an exciting way to make an *enormous* Easter egg from real eggshells! Have your students collect clean eggshells at home and bring them to class. You might also ask the school cook to save eggshells because you will need dozens of eggshells for this activity. First divide the eggshells into three batches and then dye them in three different pastel colors. Dry the shells. Place the eggshells in three different grocery bags and slightly crush them with your hands. Make an egg shape approximately 10 inches by 14 inches from the pastel construction paper, using the pattern in the border and pattern section at the end of the book. Spread glue with a paintbrush over the entire egg shape, using the same color construction paper as the color of the dyed eggshells. Have each child glue the colored cracked eggshells on the paper to form a mosaic. Continue this process until the entire egg is covered with eggshells. Let the egg dry. Cut a large egg shape from white butcher paper. Carefully apply paste to the back of each egg and place in rows to form stripes and a repeat design. Have children trace and cut out handprints from green construction paper. Curl the handprints over a pencil to form curled "handprint" grass.

Directions to Assemble

Once your eggs have dried on the butcher paper, staple the giant eggs onto a large bulletin board. (You may want to back the board with a pastel shade of butcher paper.) Staple the curled, green handprints around the egg to provide curled clumps of grass. What an enormous, elegant Easter egg you created by working together!

From *Big Bulletin Boards: A Cooperative Approach*, published by Scott, Foresman and Company. Copyright © 1991 Karen Robbins Bigler.

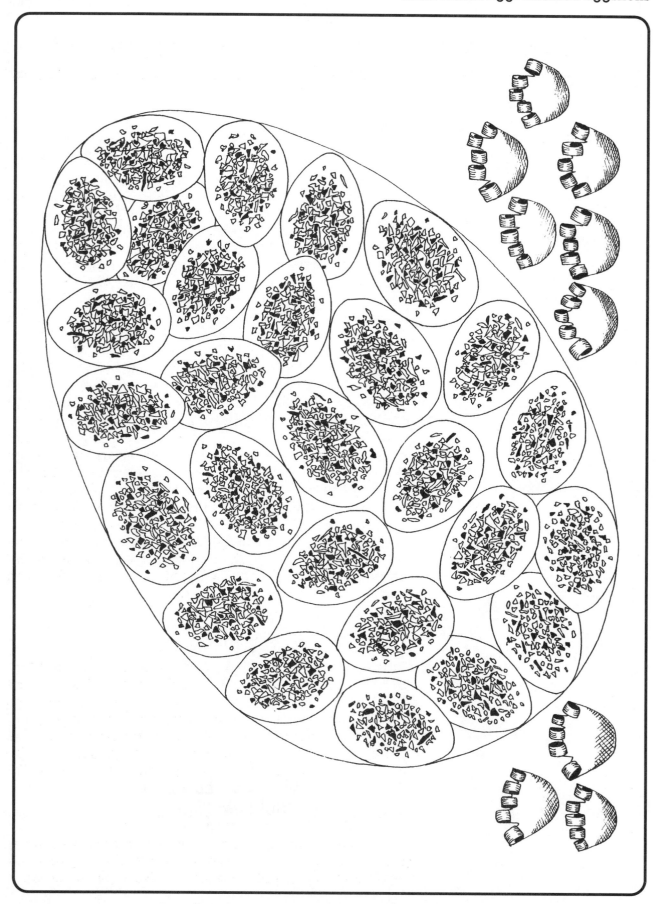

Easter Basket: Weaving/Crayon Resist

Teaching Objectives

Art:
To teach paper weaving

Physical:
To improve small muscle coordination

Language:
To teach vocabulary: *in, weaving, over, under, out*

Art:
To teach how to paint and develop creativity and imagination

Materials Needed

Construction paper, 9″ × 12″ (pink or yellow)
Butcher paper (green)
Scissors
Paper cutter (teacher to use)
Crayons
Paint (pastel color, thin wash)
Construction paper, 9″ × 12″ (white)
Egg shape pattern (tagboard)
Stapler
Paste
Pencil
Paintbrushes

Directions to Make

Paper weaving is fun to learn and easy for most children once they have caught the rhythm. Prepare in advance the 9 inch by 12 inch grids from the pink or yellow construction paper and the 1 inch by 9 inch strips from white construction paper. Choose your favorite spring colors. Teach the over and under, in and out, weaving method. For small children, use a large grid as a sample. Continue weaving until the woven grid is completed. Cut off any excess ends and paste each strip down (hiding paste underneath the paper strips). A crayon resist is a wonderful way to make elegant Easter eggs. Using a 9 inch by 12 inch sheet of white construction paper, have each child trace with a pencil around a large egg pattern on tagboard. Challenge your students to a coloring contest to create the most beautiful Easter egg in the class! By showing different designs, styles of lines, and pattern repeats on the blackboard, you can inspire creative thinking. A crayon resist will be successful only if the artist uses colors *boldly*. For this technique, children must not color lightly, because there must be enough wax from the crayon to block the paint. Emphasize to students that it is important to color *heavily* and not to use soft strokes. After students are satisfied with their designer egg, have them choose a colorful pastel paint wash to brush lightly over the crayon design. Students will be fascinated to see how the crayon resists the paint. Let the paint dry.

Directions to Assemble

Putting this giant Easter basket together is easy and fun. Simply staple the woven mats to the bulletin board, starting from the left side of the board. Position the mats carefully in rows, slightly touching each side of the mat. Cut or fold other mats in half to make the handle over the top of the basket. Fill your giant woven basket with the beautiful crayon resist Easter eggs. Happy Easter to all!

Suggestions

Other ways to design Easter eggs are: marble roll, straw blowing, string painting, sponge painting, torn paper collage, cracked eggshell collage, and tissue-paper mosaic.

May
Tulips: Handprint Cutouts

Teaching Objectives

Language:
To teach vocabulary: *flower, tulip, spring, garden, stem, leaves*

Art:
To teach how to paste, cut, and fold

Physical:
To improve small muscle coordination

Materials Needed

Construction paper (green, pink, yellow, and orange)
Scissors
Paste
Pencil
Stapler
Butcher paper (brown or rust)
Paper cutter (teacher to use)

Directions to Make

This pot of tulips will delight all mothers on Mother's Day! Have each child make a handprint tulip by tracing his or her hand with a pencil (spreading fingers wide apart) on yellow construction paper. Cut carefully on the lines and fold in the little finger and the thumb. Trace the index finger on orange paper, and place in the center of the tulip, stapling the index finger at the lower edge of the hand. With a paper cutter, cut long stems and leaves from the green construction paper and paste to the tulip.

Directions to Assemble

Cut from the brown or rust butcher paper a large, clay flowerpot to fill the lower half of the bulletin board. Tuck each individual tulip inside the pot and staple it in place. Oh, what a beautiful pot of yellow tulips that will last all month without watering! Happy Spring and Happy Mother's Day!

Note: Very young children may make the tulip by tracing a hand and leaving it flat to form a tulip that is not three-dimensional.

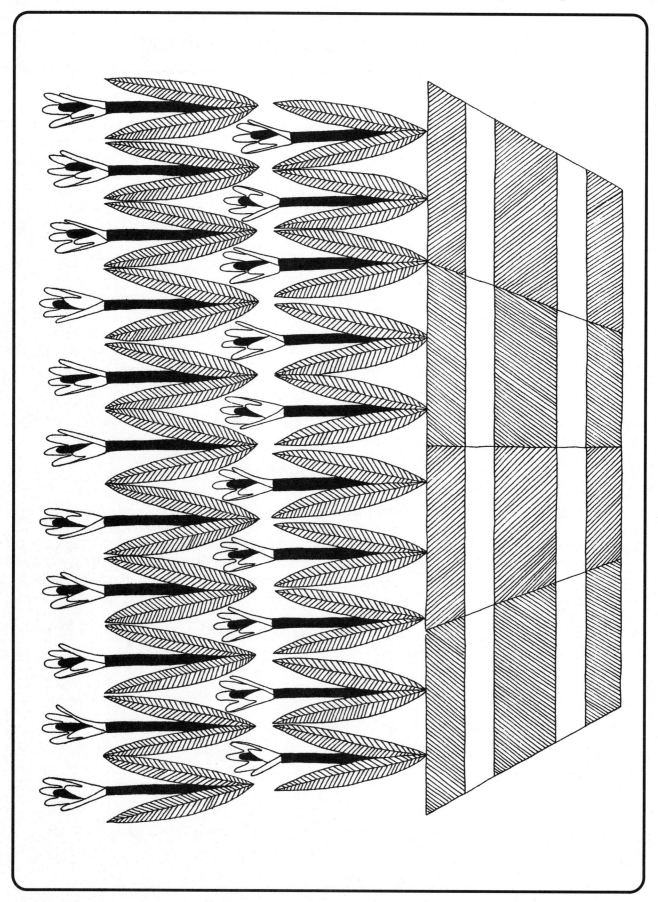

May
Rainbow: Large Paper Chains

Teaching Objectives

Language:
To teach vocabulary: *red, orange, yellow, green, blue, purple, black, and gold*

Mathematics:
To teach counting and the concepts more than, less than, bigger, shorter, longer

Physical:
To improve small muscle coordination

Art:
To make a paper-link chain

Materials Needed

Construction paper strips, 3″ × 12″ (red, orange, yellow, green, blue, and purple)
Paper cutter (teacher to use)
Butcher paper (black)
Stapler
Gold foil or Christmas wrapping paper
Cardboard

Directions to Make

To children, rainbows are fascinating and at the same time frustrating, because the children can't catch them. They will enjoy making this paper-chain rainbow while at the same time learning about colors. With a paper cutter, cut strips about 3 inches by 12 inches from the six colors of construction paper. Since paste may not hold these large strips, staplers are recommended. Staple links together to form giant paper chains.

Directions to Assemble

Plan to make two to three rows of each color depending on the size of your bulletin board. Decide the order of colors and the approximate length for each. Have a group of children cut out a black bucket and many gold-foil circles for a pot of gold at the end of the rainbow. Wrap gold-foil gift paper over cardboard circles to make the gold pieces.

Suggestions

Make a real rainbow outdoors with a garden hose by spraying water into the sunshine. Mix colored paints to show children how colors are formed (red and yellow combined make orange, blue and yellow combined make green, blue and red combined make purple). Read a book on rainbows to your class and observe the various colors that blend together.

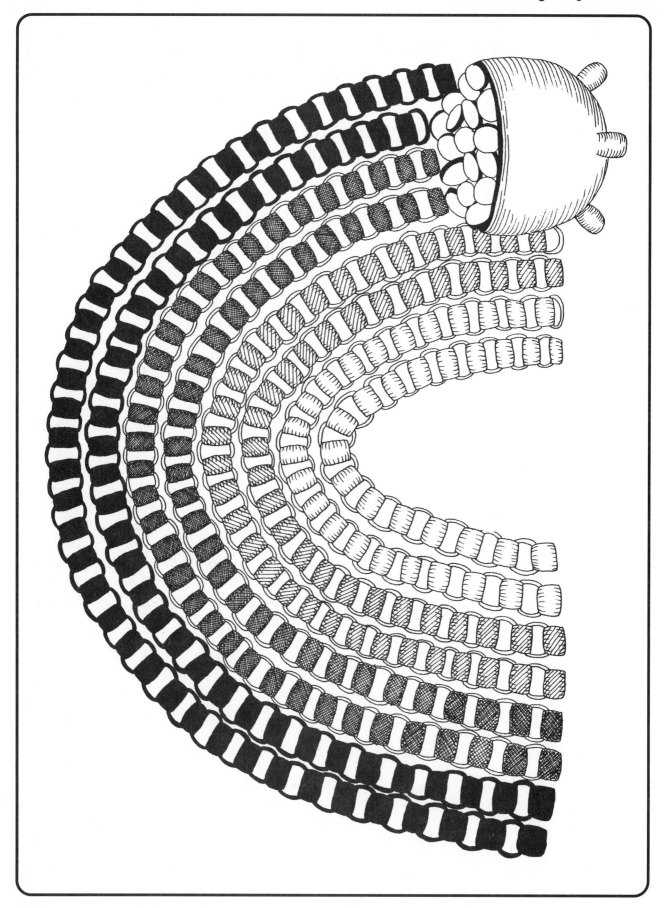

Big Beautiful Butterfly: Tissue-Paper Collage

Teaching Objectives

Art:
To teach how to cut and trace

Physical:
To improve small muscle coordination

Language:
To teach vocabulary:
butterfly, wings, antennae

Materials Needed

Construction paper (black and white)
Butcher paper (black)
Scissors
Starch (liquid)
Colored tissue-paper scraps
Tagboard
Paintbrush
White chalk
Colored marker pens
Paste
Stapler

Directions to Make

Make several tagboard butterflies from the border and pattern section at the end of the book. With white chalk, have each child trace around the butterfly pattern on the black construction paper. Then cut carefully along the chalk line. With scissors, cut small shapes from both wings, forming a delicate pattern. Lightly coat the back side of the pattern with the liquid starch, using a paintbrush. Place colored tissue squares over the cut-out holes to form a perfect butterfly pattern, and let it dry. Fold and staple the underneath portion of the body to give a three-dimensional look. Next, cut from white construction paper a white heart for the butterfly's face. Draw facial features on the heart with colored marker pens. Cut from the black butcher paper a long, narrow body, a head, and the antennae. Paste the heart-shaped head on black butcher-paper cutout.

Directions to Assemble

To assemble the butterfly, place the butterfly's long, black body and head in the center of the bulletin board. Staple to secure. Arrange the small butterflies in the form of two large wings on the left and right sides of the body, filling the entire board. Staple each wing to secure it in place. What a beautiful spring board the students have made by cooperating together!

Teaching Objectives

Language:
To teach vocabulary: *bird, beak, tail, head, body, nest*

Science:
To teach about birds, building nests, and baby birds as a sign of spring

Art:
To teach how to staple and curl paper

Physical:
To improve small muscle coordination

Materials Needed

Construction paper,
  1″ × 18″ (red, blue, brown, yellow, orange, and black)
Scissors
Stapler
Pencil
Paper cutter (teacher to use)
Pins
Macrame jute

Directions to Make

Using a paper cutter, cut six different colors of construction paper, 1 inch by 18 inches. If you want to make a "robin," place the red strip on the bottom and the blue strip on the top. Hold the strips together evenly, stapling them together at one end. With your fingers, hold the strips on the outside edge, and one by one pull up each strip evenly apart to form a head and staple them together at the neck. Next, in a downward motion, pull each strip evenly apart to form the chest. Staple the strips together, leaving the excess for the tail. Wrap each strip over a pencil to make a curly tail. You may curl some strips upward and others downward. Cut the ends into a point to make the bird's beak.

Directions to Assemble

Create a large bird's nest by filling the lower half of the bulletin board with macrame jute. Staple the strands to form a large nest. Pin the birds perching on the outside edge, sitting inside the nest, and starting to fly away.

Suggestion

Try to observe (from afar) a family of birds building a nest, or display an old nest on the science table.

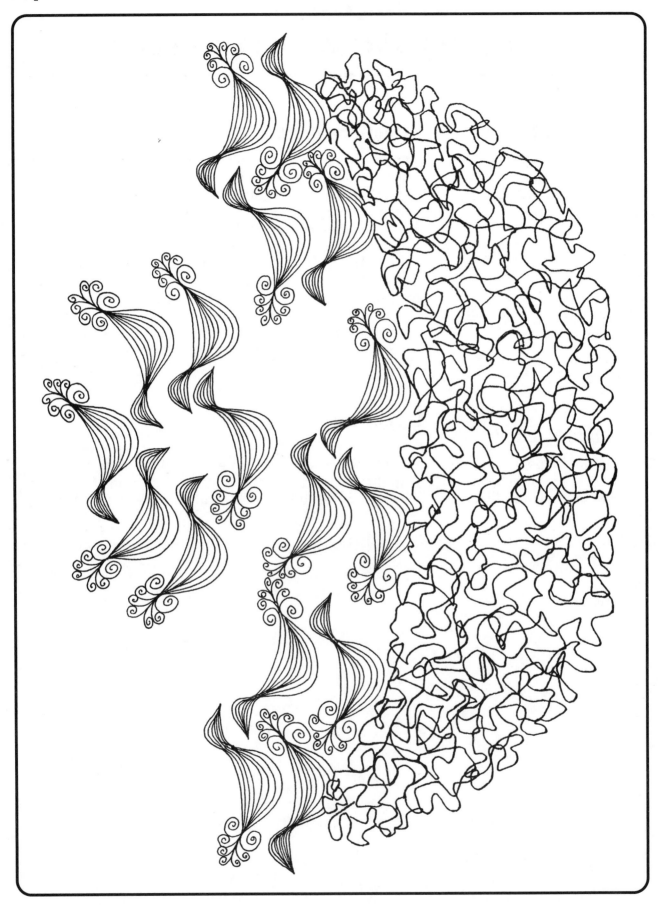

Balloon Bouquet: Stuffed Paper

Teaching Objectives

Art:
To cut; to develop creativity and imagination

Language:
To teach vocabulary:
balloon, bouquet, yarn

Physical:
To improve small motor skills

Materials Needed

Construction paper, 12″ × 18″ (variety of colors); or butcher paper (variety of colors)
Scissors
Yarn
Stapler
Newspapers
Colored marker pens

Directions to Make

A bouquet of balloons is bright and colorful. Your class will have fun creating their very own bouquet! Have each student choose a color from the construction paper or the butcher paper. Then have each student place two sheets of the same color paper together and lightly sketch the shape or image of her or his choice (heart, flower, oval, round, oblong, and so on). Holding both pieces together carefully, cut on the lines. Using the marker pens, create a design or special message. Staple close to the edge both pieces of paper, leaving an open space for stuffing. Crumple newspaper and poke it inside the open space to puff the balloon slightly. Finish by stapling the edges of the open space together and attaching yarn at the bottom of the balloon.

Directions to Assemble

Place the children's colorful puffed balloons on the bulletin board, stapling them in place. Arrange them in a bouquet, tying the yarn streamers together at the bottom with a bow. Enjoy this beautiful bouquet all month long. How many balloons are there all together? How many are the same color? How many are the same shape? You and your students can be glad that you put together such a pretty balloon bouquet!

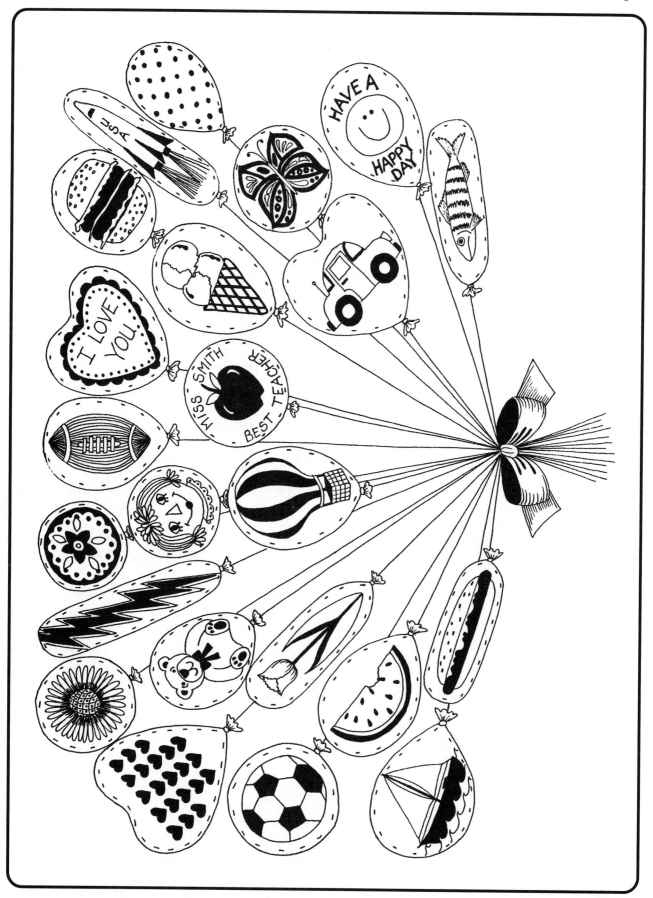

Teaching Objectives

Art:
To introduce the crayon resist technique; to develop creativity and imagination; to teach painting, using the proper strokes

Language:
To teach vocabulary: *fish, bowl, seaweed*

Physical:
To improve small muscle coordination

Materials Needed

Large sheet of butcher paper (white)
Thin blue paint (wash)
Crayons
A book about fish or fish pattern on page 92
Tape
Masking tape
Paintbrush
Stapler

Directions to Make

Read a book on fish to the children, showing pictures of the many varieties of fish. Also, refer to the fish pattern in the border and pattern section at the back of the book.

Cut a large piece of white butcher paper into the shape of a large fishbowl—big enough to fill the entire bulletin board. If necessary, tape the center seam together with masking tape on the back side. After placing the paper on a large table, have the children come in small groups, each to color a special fish of his or her choice, pebbles, and seaweed in the fishbowl. Remind children to press hard not lightly, as they color. The wax from the crayons must resist the paint wash. When all the children have colored a fish, pebbles, and seaweed, have them apply a thin blue wash of paint over the entire piece. Children may come in small groups once again to take turns painting. Let the paint dry.

Directions to Assemble

When the paint has dried, staple the fishbowl onto the bulletin board. Have the class come to the board and count the number of different fish drawn. How many are alike? Discuss the different colors and kinds of fish that are represented.

Suggestion

Following the directions just given, you may also make the ocean by cutting butcher paper to fill the entire bulletin board. Have students color a variety of sea animals, plants, and rocks, as well as a sunken ship and a scuba diver. This is a creative way to prepare for summer fun at the beach!

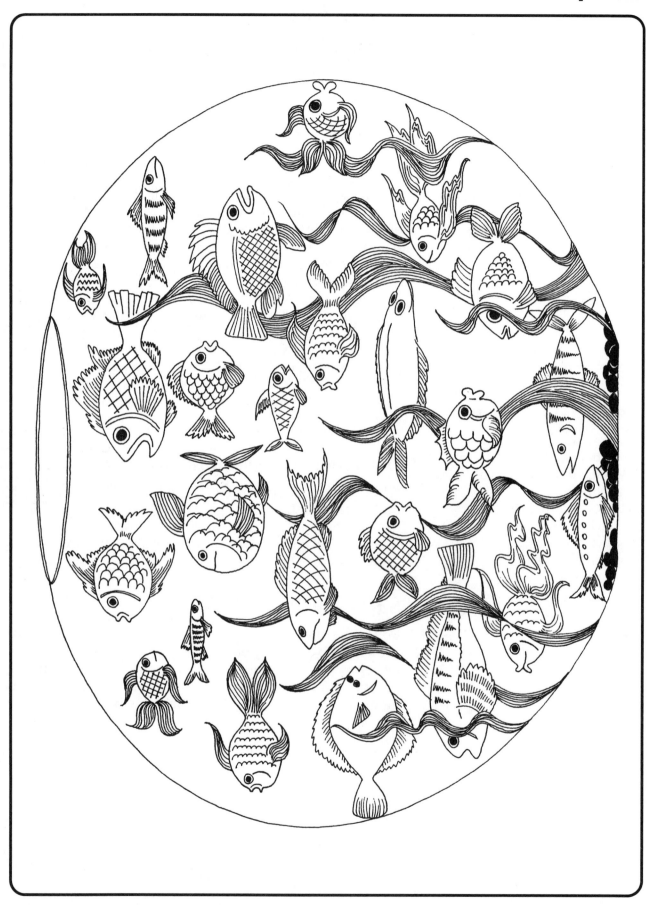

From *Big Bulletin Boards: A Cooperative Approach,* published by Scott, Foresman and Company. Copyright © 1991 Karen Robbins Bigler.

June/Summer
A Super Summer:
Styrofoam Cut and Color

Teaching Objectives

Language:
To discuss favorite flavors of ice cream

Physical:
To improve small motor skills

Art:
To cut; to develop creativity

Language:
To teach color vocabulary: *brown, yellow, pink, orange, green*

Materials Needed

Butcher paper (color of your choice)
Extra-large Styrofoam meat trays
Magic markers
Scissors
Pins

Directions to Make

To make some super ice-cream cones, collect extra-large size Styrofoam meat trays. Wash and dry the trays. With scissors, cut a large half circle from each tray to form the ice-cream scoops. Cut off the outside edge from the Styrofoam trays to be used for the waffle cones. Using magic markers, color the smooth side of the Styrofoam half circles to make your favorite ice cream. Color the patterned side of the tray to make the waffle cone, with a cream-colored marker. Use the ice-cream cone pattern in the border and pattern section at the end of the book for the cones.

Directions to Assemble

Have fun assembling the ice-cream cones by first placing them on the background paper. Divide the bulletin board into thirds, and pin some waffle cones on the lowest third of the board. Pin scoops of ice cream on top of each cone, keeping the row straight. Repeat these steps to form the second and the third rows of cones. What a great way to have a super summer!

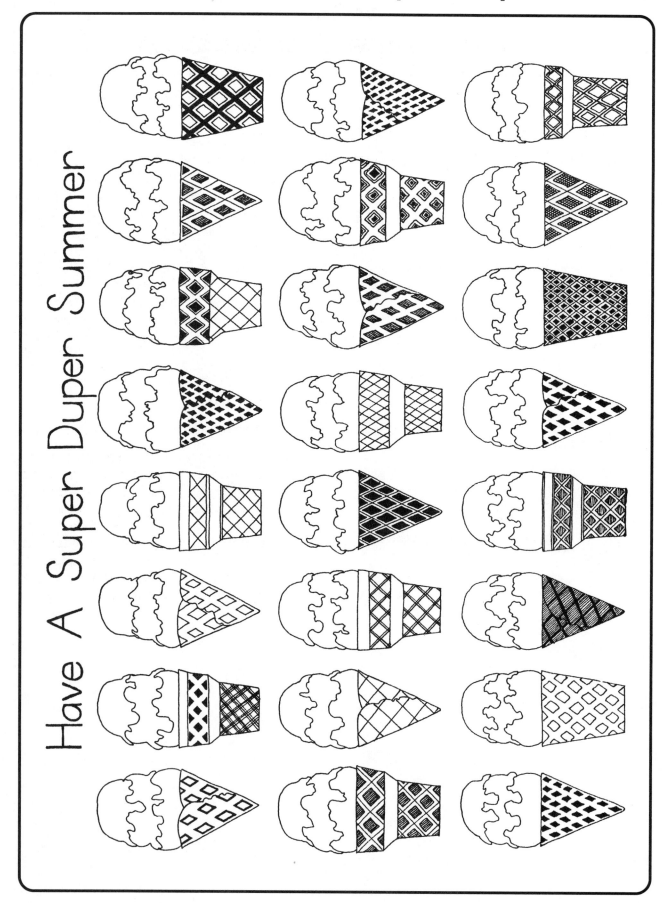

Have A Super Duper Summer

June/Summer
Mr. Sunshine: Summer Goals

Teaching Objectives

Social:
To make goals for the summer vacation

Language:
To provide penmanship and spelling lessons; to develop writing skills

Speech:
To teach communication and discussion skills

Reading:
To provide reading material

Materials Needed

Butcher paper strips approximately 4″ × 36″ (yellow)
Large butcher paper (yellow and white)
Paper cutter (teacher to use)
Magic markers (assorted colors)
Scissors
Pens or pencils

Directions to Make

School is almost out, and what will students do this summer? Help your students set some goals, and see how many they can accomplish. Here is a great way to collect a multitude of ideas to prevent summer boredom and stimulate summertime fun! Cut long, rectangular strips approximately 4 inches by 36 inches from the yellow butcher paper. With a marker pen, write each student's name at the top of a strip. Have a class discussion of summer activities, plans, and ideas that the students hope to participate in. List these ideas on the blackboard. Have the students make their own list of summer plans, writing neatly as possible on the yellow butcher paper strips. Cut from the large butcher paper a big circle, and draw in a happy face, using colored marker pens.

Directions to Assemble

Cover the bulletin board with white background paper, if needed. Staple the happy face in the center and attach each strip at equal distance apart, creating a sun with rays. Then enjoy reading each student's list of ideas for a super summer vacation. At the end of the month, disassemble the sun, and give each child her or his list on the last day of school. Suggest that the student place it in her or his room, to refer to when the student is bored and can't think of anything to do. Happy summer vacation!

From *Big Bulletin Boards: A Cooperative Approach*, published by Scott, Foresman and Company. Copyright © 1991 Karen Robbins Bigler.

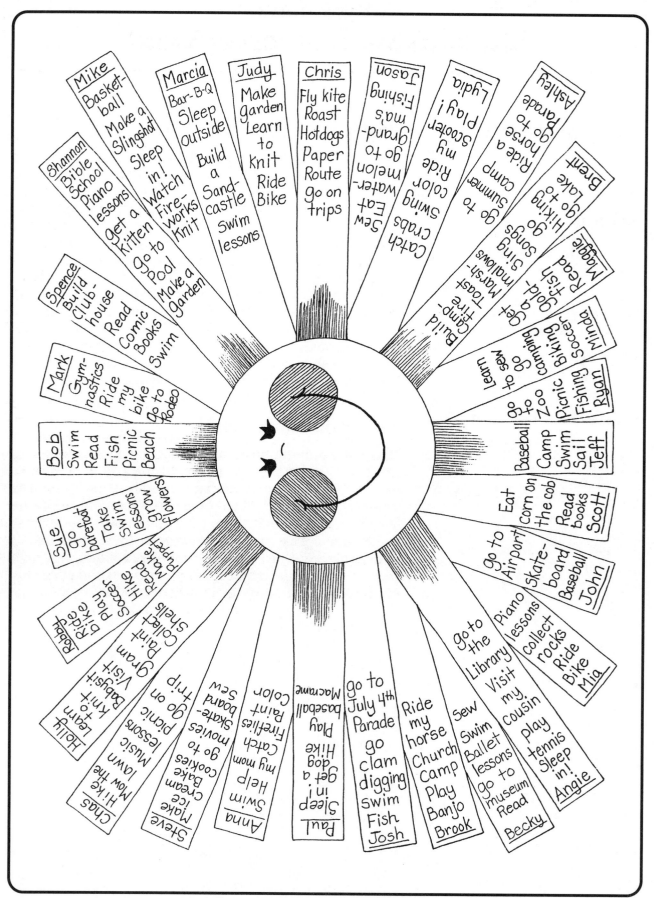

June/Summer
Musical Notes: Tissue Twist

Teaching Objectives

Music:
To teach beginning music (staff, treble clef, notes, lines, spaces, bars)

Language:
To teach music vocabulary: *notes, staff, space, beats, signature*

Physical:
To improve small muscle coordination

Materials Needed

Black yarn
Tissue paper (black)
Tagboard notes
Paste
Construction paper (black)
Pencil
Stapler
Butcher paper

Directions to Make

Create your own class song, and teach the basics of music with this musical bulletin board. First, make the tagboard notes, using the pattern in the border and pattern section at the end of the book. Have each student choose a note, and then trace and cut it from the tagboard. Place the eraser end of the pencil in the center of a black tissue square, and pinch the tissue together. Dab it into the paste and then place on a tagboard note. Continue this process, placing each piece of tissue close together until the tagboard is completely covered. Discuss the note value and the number of beats with each child.

Directions to Assemble

Cover the entire bulletin board with a background paper of your choice. Decide whether you want to compose your own song or to copy an existing one. Staple five straight parallel lines of black yarn across the top of the board, each at an equal distance apart. Leave about 10 inches, and then staple five more straight parallel lines of yarn at the center of the board. Leave another 10 inches or so and attach five lines of yarn close to the bottom. Cut shorter pieces of yarn, and then staple them to form measures at equal distances apart. Pin or staple each student's note either on a line or a space. Have students sing or play instruments such as the tambourine, cymbals, sticks, triangle, drums, and bells to the class tune that you composed together!

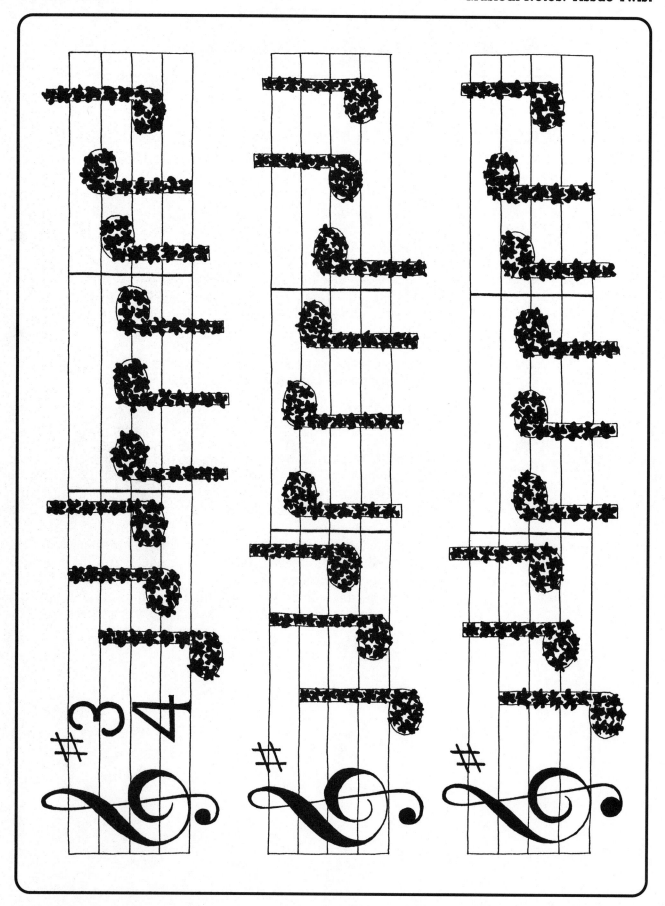

Borders and Patterns for Bulletin Boards

The borders that follow may be made quickly and easily by your class to add a finished touch to the bulletin boards described in this book. All younger children will enjoy the simple method of folding construction paper, tracing around the patterns, and cutting along the outline edge. How delighted they will be when they unfold their paper to find a row of happy holiday friends!

Use the simple borders, or create your own, to enhance the bulletin boards each month. Staple the children's cutout borders close together to outline the big, cooperative bulletin board. Or trim all the boards in the classroom to give an attractive, uniform look. Not only will your students have fun making the borders, they will also be proud of the pleasing atmosphere they helped create by working together.

The patterns that follow have been prepared for your convenience. Simply enlarge them on a photocopying machine or opaque projector to the size of your choice. Trace the patterns onto cardboard and then cut out forms for patterns to make the bulletin boards within the book. This quick and easy method will help even the most uncreative teacher to prepare the items that are required for the students to create their bulletin boards in the classroom. With this time-saving device, all the bulletin boards can be made quickly and successfully throughout the year. Good luck making big bulletin boards together with your students!

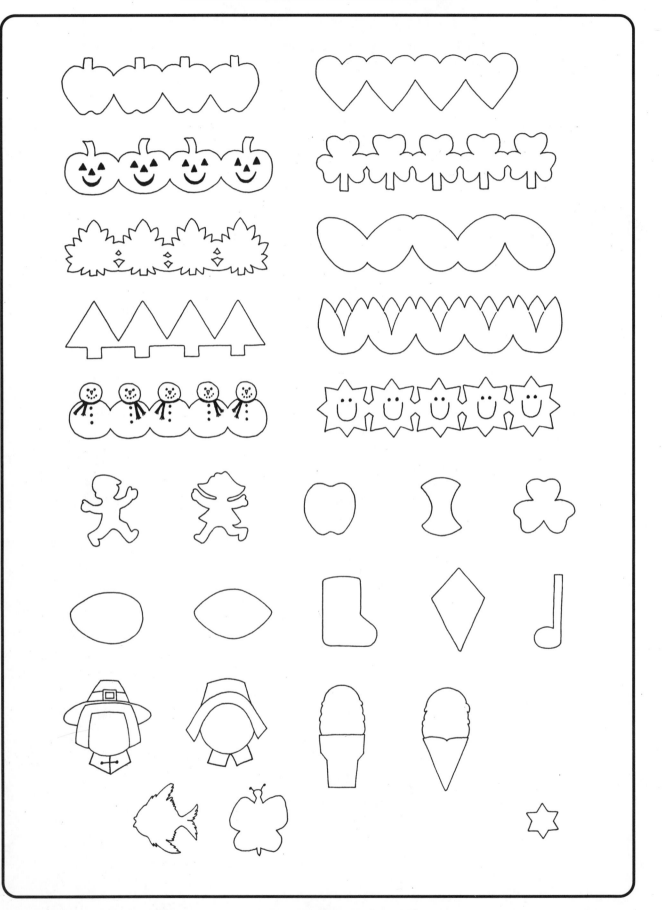